**EPICS**

# CLIMATE CHANGE
## *and* SOCIETY

Raymond S. Bradley
and Norman Law

*Series Editor*
Michael Witherick

Published in 2001 by:
Nelson Thornes Ltd
Delta Place
27 Bath Road
CHELTENHAM
GL53 7TH
United Kingdom

01 02 03 04 05 / 10 9 8 7 6 5 4 3 2 1

A catalogue record for this book is available from the British Library

ISBN 0 7487 5823 2

Illustrations and page make-up by Multiplex Techniques Ltd

Printed and bound in Great Britain by Martins The Printers Ltd

**Acknowledgements**
With thanks to the following for permission to reproduce photographs and other copyright material in this book:

Associated Press, Figs 1.4, 8.2
Corel, Figs 7.3, 7.4, 7.5
Images of Africa Photobank, Fig 1.1
Oxford Scientific Films, Fig 3.4
Paleographic Maps by Christopher R. Scotese, Paleomap Project, University of Texas at Arlington, Fig 4.1
RSPB, Fig 7.2
Jorgen Schytte/Still Pictures, Fig 6.9

*The Times*, October 26, 2000, Fig 4.7; Friends of the Earth, Fig 8.5, (from *Energy Without End*, M. Flood, 1991)

Every effort has been made to contact copyright holders. The publishers apologise to anyone whose rights have been inadvertently overlooked, and will be happy to rectify any errors or omissions.

# Contents

# Setting the scene

## Changing climates

'Global warming' is frequently in the news nowadays. It has become a major topic of conversation throughout the world but, as with many environmental issues, people are often confused by myths and half-truths. In order to explode those myths and explore the truth, this book will address a range of important questions:

- How have climates varied in the past?
- To what extent is global warming just a part of 'normal' climatic change?
- Can human activity really affect global climate?
- If it does, are all the effects bad, or are there some benefits?
- What will our climate be like in the future?
- If people are affecting global climate, is there anything we can do to reduce the impact?
- Should we even bother?

By addressing these questions, this book will enable you to become better informed and approach a conversation on global warming and climatic change with more confidence.

## The past

The remarkable thing about the cave paintings from north-west Sudan (**1.1**) is not that they have lasted in such a fresh condition for well over 6000 years. Rather, it is that they depict an extremely rich biodiversity in an area that is now one of the most inhospitable deserts on Earth. Fossil bones found in the area show that, until around 6000 years ago, what is now part of the arid southeastern Sahara was considerably wetter, and supported a savanna ecosystem with giraffes, elephants, lions, antelopes, monkeys, ostriches and a wide array of other species. It was also a flourishing agricultural area, where domestic cattle were raised and fishing took place in lakes and rivers. Today, in this utterly arid environment, it is hard to imagine such activities, yet these cave paintings vividly testify to the dramatic changes in climate that have taken place in this relatively short period of time.

In fact, climatic changes have taken place repeatedly throughout the Earth's history. In some regions, this has involved major changes in rainfall and hydrology. In other places, temperature changes have led to glaciations and the growth of ice sheets. Much of the world's population now lives in

**Figure 1.1** During the period from 11 000 to 5500 years ago, the climate of the Sahara was much wetter than today. This enabled grazing animals to live there, and for people to occupy the region. Today, evidence of this former wet period is vividly seen in the markings on rock walls, depicting animals that can no longer survive in this extremely arid region

these same locations. Climatic changes are indeed a normal feature of our environment. By studying the records of how climates have changed, we can begin to understand why they changed. This, in turn, helps us to understand the changes that are happening today. It also helps us to put these changes in perspective, so we can then tell whether they are 'normal' or beyond what we might expect as a result of 'natural' change.

## The present

The world's climate has been unusually disturbed in recent years. Some examples from 1999 weather data reveal a catalogue of record-breaking events. For instance, southern India had the worst heat wave in 50 years, leaving over 4000 people dead. Saudi Arabia's heat wave was the worst in 110 years. New York had its first ever case of mosquito-borne encephalitis. This is an extremely dangerous disease associated with conditions that are suitable for the insect to multiply, conditions that usually only exist much further south (especially a wet spring followed by a hot summer). Northern Mexico had its worst drought in 70 years, and so on. Of course, there are always record-breaking weather events somewhere in the world, but the large number of recent extremes has led some to wonder whether the Earth is entering a period of climatic instability.

The Earth's climate has never been entirely stable (**1.2**). It has varied many times in the past, so we should not be surprised that we seem to be living through another such period now. To what extent are the changes of recent years part of the normal variation of climate over time or the result of human activity? What sort of changes will affect us in the future and how can we adapt to them? We still do not understand all of the parameters that affect climate, so the prediction of future changes remains problematical.

The current consensus of opinion is that human activity has so altered the balance of the global climate machine that it is beginning to become unstable. Human interference is superimposed on natural processes, such

**Figure 1.2** A schematic diagram illustrating climatic fluctuations, at time-scales ranging from the past 100 years (lowest panel) to the past 1000 years (second panel) to the past 10 000 years and so on, to the past million years (top panel)

Each successive panel, from the back to the front, is an expanded version (expanded by a factor of ten) of one-tenth of the previous column. In this way, the short-term climatic variations that we have clear evidence for in recent years are 'nested' within the longer-term changes of earlier epochs. Note that the temperature scale (representing global mean annual temperature) is the same on all panels. This demonstrates that temperature changes over the past 100 years (lowest panel) have been minor compared to changes over long periods of time. Such changes have occurred throughout history, but they are lost in the noise of the longer-term climatic record; only the largest changes are detectable as we look far back in time.

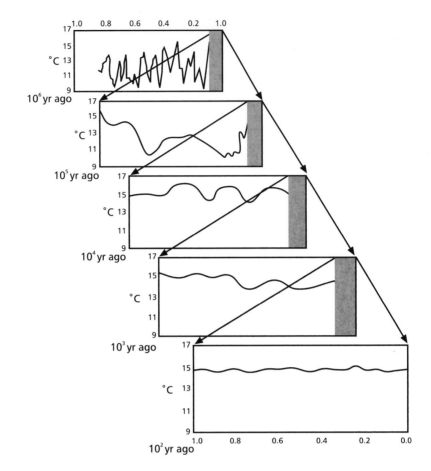

as those that led to the decline of the Saharan civilisation mentioned above. The balance of probability is that climate is indeed changing as a result of human activities. Most climatologists certainly think in this way, although there is still much debate about how the changes will affect different regions in the future. Will we soon see headlines like those in **1.3**?

The main rules that govern the global climate system are reasonably well understood, so computer models of world climate are becoming ever more accurate. As they do so, we will be able to see exactly what lies in store for us. In the meantime, it would be a good idea to plan for change, so that society can cope with what actually occurs.

## The future

At the stroke of midnight on 1 January 2000, Millennium Island had a few minutes of fame (**1.4**). It was the first place on Earth to enter the new millennium. But will it be there for much longer? Kiribati is an archipelago in the South Pacific, whose mean height above sea level is less than 1 m. The inhabitants briefly became the centre of world attention as they welcomed in a new era, but the nation's leader took the opportunity to remind the rest of the world of his country's perilous state. He said that as

**Figure 1.3** Are these the headlines that we will have to get used to reading in future newspapers? In 2000 there were more weather-related headlines than there had been for many years. How frequent will they be by 2025 when, according to many scientists, global warming will have disrupted world weather patterns?

HOTTEST SUMMER EVER
12 October 2025

TEMPERATURES SOAR
25 July 2050

PHEW! WHAT A SCORCHER!
10 August 2100

HIGHEST JUNE RAIN TOTAL
1 July 2008

"PERFECT STORM" HITS SOUTHWEST
22 December 2157

climate warming leads to the melting of the polar ice-caps and a consequent rise in sea level, some countries would be mildly inconvenienced while others would be badly affected. But Kiribati could well disappear altogether.

**Figure 1.4** The midnight celebrations on Millennium Island, 1 January 2000

# About this book

## Content and structure

This book starts by explaining how the global climate system works (**Chapter 2**), and then examines the techniques used to establish what climates were like in the past (**Chapter 3**) and why they changed (**Chapter 4**). **Chapter 5** looks in more detail at the current climate and the fluctuations that seem to have occurred in recent years, and explores the reasons for these fluctuations. The effects of these and possible future changes in climate on the environment and on people are investigated in **Chapter 6** and **Chapter 7** respectively. Sea-level rise is one of the outcomes of higher global mean temperatures that seems to have few positive benefits. However, not all of the consequences of global warming will be as disastrous as those that may befall Kiribati. For example, some areas will be able to grow a wider variety of crops; some areas that currently suffer frequent droughts will have more rainfall; and yet others will enjoy climatic changes that will allow them to develop their tourist industry. Uncertainties about the balance between the 'benefits' and the detrimental effects of global warming make it difficult for policy-makers to deal with the issue. In **Chapter 8**, a range of options that are currently being considered to address the problem is examined. Overall, this book should help you to achieve an understanding of climatic change and the resulting challenges that we all face.

## Sources

Throughout the book, you will find references to various websites that give more information about the various topics mentioned. Use these to explore those issues that are of particular interest to you. In some cases, the sites provide maps and graphs – and even videos – that you should look at to learn more about a subject. As a general starting-point, look at the website for a book on *Paleoclimatology* by Raymond S. Bradley and follow the links in that. The address is:

http://www.geo.umass.edu/climate/paleo/html/

Warning! The websites given throughout the book are generally governmental or academic sites that have been prepared by experts on each subject, and carefully checked for accuracy by the authors. You should be aware that many websites are set up by special-interest groups that have their own agendas, and they may therefore be quite biased. Often, the authors are not specialists and may be unfamiliar with current research on the topic. Use the World Wide Web carefully and be aware of these possible problems. Always report where you found the information and check it against other sites.

## Review

1 As you study geography, keep a world climate log. Cut out and keep news items of unusual weather events, or of the consequences of climatic change.

There are many articles on climatic change and its effect on society, and a back catalogue can often be found by logging on to electronic versions of newspapers such as *The Guardian* (http://www.guardian.co.uk), *The Times* (http://www.the-times.co.uk) or *The Independent* (http://www.independent.co.uk). News organisations also have excellent electronic resources: see the BBC World Service (http://www.bbc.co.uk/worldservice) and CNN (http://www.cnn.com).

Make notes about any such events that might be mentioned on the TV or the radio. Detailed notes of actual events will enable you to illustrate your examination answers or project work with interesting and completely up-to-date examples that will certainly get you extra credit.

2 The data in **1.5** gives actual recorded temperatures for Plymouth (Massachusetts, USA) over the past 100 years. Each value is the annual average for a five-year period. Calculate a three-value running mean and plot these numbers together with the original five-year averages on a graph. Describe the changes that you see. Compare these data with those for the entire Earth in **1.2** and then comment on the similarities and differences.

**Figure 1.5** Temperature data for Plymouth, Massachusetts (years and temperatures in degrees Celsius)

| | | | | | | | | | | | |
|---|---|---|---|---|---|---|---|---|---|---|---|
| 1891 | 16.2 | 1908 | 16.2 | 1925 | 16.6 | 1942 | 15.6 | 1959 | 16.8 | 1976 | 17.9 |
| 1892 | 15.4 | 1909 | 15.7 | 1926 | 17.9 | 1943 | 16.5 | 1960 | 15.2 | 1977 | 16.6 |
| 1893 | 16.4 | 1910 | 14.9 | 1927 | 16.3 | 1944 | 15.6 | 1961 | 15.7 | 1978 | 14.7 |
| 1894 | 14.9 | 1911 | 18.8 | 1928 | 16.8 | 1945 | 15.8 | 1962 | 15.3 | 1979 | 16.3 |
| 1895 | 15.0 | 1912 | 16.7 | 1929 | 16.4 | 1946 | 15.5 | 1963 | 14.9 | 1980 | 14.7 |
| 1896 | 16.3 | 1913 | 16.0 | 1930 | 15.7 | 1947 | 16.2 | 1964 | 15.9 | 1981 | 15.9 |
| 1897 | 17.0 | 1914 | 15.9 | 1931 | 14.9 | 1948 | 15.7 | 1965 | 14.5 | 1982 | 16.9 |
| 1898 | 16.3 | 1915 | 15.0 | 1932 | 15.5 | 1949 | 17.4 | 1966 | 15.8 | 1983 | 19.8 |
| 1899 | 16.9 | 1916 | 15.9 | 1933 | 16.8 | 1950 | 15.7 | 1967 | 15.9 | 1984 | 16.8 |
| 1900 | 16.8 | 1917 | 16.6 | 1934 | 18.4 | 1951 | 16.4 | 1968 | 15.3 | 1985 | 16.2 |
| 1901 | 17.6 | 1918 | 16.1 | 1935 | 17.3 | 1952 | 16.7 | 1969 | 16.2 | 1986 | 15.6 |
| 1902 | 15.2 | 1919 | 15.2 | 1936 | 15.0 | 1953 | 15.6 | 1970 | 15.3 | 1987 | 16.5 |
| 1903 | 15.5 | 1920 | 14.7 | 1937 | 15.9 | 1954 | 13.9 | 1971 | 17.8 | 1988 | 14.7 |
| 1904 | 16.8 | 1921 | 18.7 | 1938 | 14.6 | 1955 | 17.9 | 1972 | 15.6 | 1989 | 19.1 |
| 1905 | 17.2 | 1922 | 14.1 | 1939 | 14.6 | 1956 | 15.4 | 1973 | 15.3 | 1990 | 17.1 |
| 1906 | 15.6 | 1923 | 17.9 | 1940 | 15.1 | 1957 | 16.8 | 1974 | 14.9 | | |
| 1907 | 14.8 | 1924 | 15.2 | 1941 | 16.3 | 1958 | 15.4 | 1975 | 17.0 | | |

## Enquiry

In this book you will find a lot of graphs of temperature, precipitation and carbon dioxide concentration plotted against time. Many of the individual plots are mean values. A *mean* is what is often referred to imprecisely as an 'average'. It is derived from summing the values for a number of readings and dividing by that number. This same technique can be used in a modified form to give an idea of the trend behind a time series of data. This technique is known as *running, or moving, means*. As an example, the data set shown in **1.6** would, if plotted as individual readings, yield a graph with peaks and troughs. To find the trend and begin to understand what has happened over the whole period of the readings, we need to smooth out these extremes, and we can do this by computing 'running means'.

**Figure 1.6** A data set of means

| Month | 1 | 2 | 3 | 4 | 5 | 6 | 7 | 8 | 9 | 10 |
|---|---|---|---|---|---|---|---|---|---|---|
| Mean | 10 | 15 | 8 | 12 | 16 | 10 | 12 | 15 | 12 | 16 |
| Running three-value means | – | 11 | 11.7 | | | | | | | |

To find the first three-value mean, for months 1, 2 and 3, add the three means together and divide by the number of readings. In this case, the calculation is as follows:

Add: 10 + 15 + 8 = 33
Divide: 33 ÷ 3 = 11

This value is entered into the grid square relating to the central point (i.e. under reading 2).

To find the next three-value running mean, drop the first monthly mean (10) and add in the fourth (12). Perform exactly the same procedure and find the mean, which should be entered into the grid under reading 3. This time, the calculation is as follows:

Add: 15 + 8 + 12 = 35
Divide: 35 ÷ 3 = 11.7

Continue like this until all of the values have been used.

Although this describes how to compute three-value running means, a very similar procedure can be used for any number of values over two. The most commonly used are five- and seven-value running means.

1 Look at the readings in **1.6**. Try to describe the trend shown by the readings over the ten months. What problems are there with this visual interpretation?
2 Now compute all of the three-value running means, following the procedure described above.
3 Plot the data on a graph, showing actual readings in one colour and three-value running means in another.
4 Now describe the trend shown by your three-value running means.
5 Why might trend lines be particularly useful on graphs of temperature records that cover periods of 50 years?

# Global climate

## Building a picture of climate

When the Pilgrim Fathers left England in the 17th century to settle in North America, they took with them more than the basic necessities for a new colony. They also took their collective experiences of life in England, including English weather. Having grown up on the Atlantic edge of Europe, they had built up a mental picture of what the weather in their villages and towns was like. In effect, they had accumulated a large sample of weather 'experiences' that would have enabled them to describe what a typical winter or summer might be like, what extremes might be expected, and so on. Such a large sample of weather experiences provided them with a picture of the climate of the areas that they were leaving behind.

In common usage, **climate** is a perceptual summary of the everyday weather events in an area. It refers to the overall range of weather conditions likely to be experienced there over a period of time. When the Pilgrim Fathers arrived in New England, the experience of weather in their strange new world would have been quite different: in the summer, temperatures would have been higher and conditions more humid, with thunderstorms common; while the winters would have been much colder, with more snow, and causing lakes and ponds to freeze. Over time, they might have experienced occasional hurricanes or the severe winter storms known as 'Nor-Easters' – and perhaps even a rare tornado. Eventually, these experiences would provide them with a mental picture of the climate of New England, to compare with the English climate that they left behind.

Today, meteorologists and volunteer observers carefully measure many aspects of the weather: pressure, temperature, humidity, solar radiation, precipitation, wind speed and direction. These data are compiled by national weather centres so that day-to-day weather conditions are well known and the long-term conditions in each region are easily studied. This has enabled scientists to recognise patterns of climate that different regions have in common, and to understand the factors responsible for these similarities and differences. To the scientific community, **climate** is a statistical summary of all weather, including **anomalies** (unusual happenings) over at least 30 years.

Measurements made over many decades also show that climates are not constant over time. The climate of New England that the Pilgrim Fathers first experienced in the 17th century was different (for example, colder with more snowfall in the winters) than the climate of New England today.

Changes in climate have been going on throughout the history of the Earth, due to natural factors such as:

- changes in the energy emitted by the Sun
- slight changes in the position of the Earth in relation to the Sun
- explosive volcanic eruptions and other effects.

These are known as **forcing factors** and are discussed more fully in **Chapter 3**. More recently, people have changed the composition of the atmosphere by burning fossil fuels at a tremendous rate, and by altering the vegetation cover over large areas. These human changes are now so rapid and so large that they threaten to overwhelm the natural causes of climatic change within the next 100 years.

## Review

1 Write your own definition of **climate**.

2 Review **2.1**. The terms referred to in this diagram are explained in the book. Make a copy of the diagram and then compile a key beneath it to explain each of the terms shown.

3 Explain why the burning of fossil fuels affects the Earth's temperature.

# The global climate system

Although climate is often thought of as just something to do with the atmosphere, the factors that control climate are much more complicated than that. The Earth's climate is the result of interactions between several different systems (**2.1**):

- the atmosphere
- the oceans
- the land surface
- the cryosphere (the snow- and ice-covered parts of the world)
- the biosphere.

Together, these make up the overall climate system. Each of these subsystems plays an important role in determining the climate of the Earth as a whole, and that of different locations around the world.

## The atmosphere

Of the five main subsystems, the atmosphere is the most variable and it responds most rapidly to external influences. The composition of the atmosphere – in particular, how much carbon dioxide is in the air – is very important for global climate. Carbon dioxide allows short-wave radiation (energy) from the Sun to pass through it, but when that energy is absorbed

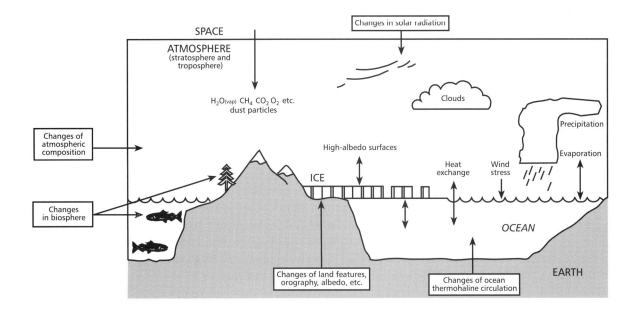

**Figure 2.1** Major components of the global climate system. Feedbacks between various components play an important role in climate variations

at the Earth's surface, it is re-radiated back to space at longer (infra-red) wavelengths. Carbon dioxide absorbs this long-wave radiation, causing the temperature of the atmosphere to rise. This gas helps to retain radiation that would otherwise escape into space, and so helps to keep the Earth's surface warm. This is known as the **greenhouse effect (2.2)**.

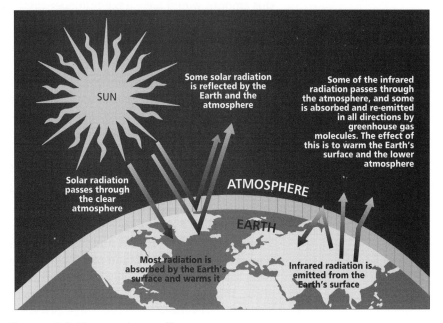

**Figure 2.2** The greenhouse effect

This diagram shows the basic underlying cause of global warming. The 'greenhouse gases' that decrease the ability of infrared radiation to escape from the Earth's atmosphere continue to build up, largely due to the burning of fossil fuels. What will happen if no action is taken to cut down the emission of gases such as carbon dioxide?

Without the greenhouse effect of carbon dioxide (plus other important 'greenhouse' gases, such as methane and water vapour), life would not exist on Earth, because the incoming solar radiation would simply be radiated back into space. On the other hand, life has evolved on Earth over geological time and has contributed to maintaining carbon dioxide levels in the atmosphere. Hundreds of millions of years ago, carbon dioxide levels in the atmosphere were higher, and evolving organisms helped to reduce those levels by converting the gas (through photosynthesis) into plant tissue. Atmospheric carbon dioxide levels still vary, from glacial to interglacial times (as discussed in **Chapter 3**), but it seems that the Earth has come to a sort of balance over long periods of geological time. Only in the past century has this balance been disrupted by the burning of fossil fuels (putting old stores of carbon from past geological periods back into the atmosphere) and by the production of industrial gases, such as chlorofluorocarbons, that strongly absorb long-wave radiation. The implications of this are discussed in **Chapter 5**.

## The oceans

The oceans are a much more sluggish component of the global climate system than the atmosphere. The surface layers of the ocean respond more slowly to external influences, and it may take centuries for significant changes to occur in the deep oceans. The oceans also play a vital role in controlling atmospheric carbon dioxide levels. They contain very large quantities of carbon dioxide ($CO_2$), dissolved in the water. Any change in this amount would have a big influence on the greenhouse effect and the world's climate.

Because water has a much higher heat capacity than air, the oceans store very large quantities of energy and act as a buffer, damping out large seasonal changes of temperature. On a large scale, this is the reason why there is a much smaller seasonal change in temperature over the Southern Hemisphere (which is mostly oceanic) compared with the Northern Hemisphere (which is dominated by continental land masses). On a smaller scale, closeness to the ocean is one of the most important factors affecting the climate of a region, along with the latitude and altitude.

Today, the oceans cover 71 per cent of the Earth's surface and hence play an enormously important role in the energy balance of the Earth. Your atlas will show you that the oceans are most extensive in the Southern Hemisphere, between 30°S and 70°S, and least extensive in the zones between 50°N and 70°N, and poleward of 70°S. Of course, it has not always been like that. Over geological time, as the continental plates have moved about, this picture has been different, changing the climates of individual locations as well as that of the Earth as a whole. As the continents have moved towards the poles, the frequency of glaciations has increased, because changes in the energy received from the Sun (due to changes in the Earth's position – see **Chapter 4**) have allowed ice sheets to grow on the land. Similarly, mountain-building episodes (**orogenies**) have had major effects on the global climate in the past, by changing the airflow over the Earth's surface.

## The land surface

On land, plate movements and mountain-building are major long-term causes of climatic change. However, explosive volcanic eruptions can have important short-term effects on climate, by throwing large amounts of dust and gas (such as sulphur dioxide) into the upper atmosphere (the **stratosphere**). Once there, this dust and gas can be quickly spread around the world by high-level winds. The volcanic dust particles (and the sulphuric acid produced when the sulphur gas dissolves in water droplets) interfere with the incoming solar energy, leading to cooling at the Earth's surface.

## Case study: The effects of volcanic eruptions on climate

The eruption, in 1815, of Tambora – an Indonesian volcano – led to a worldwide disruption in climate. In New England during the summer of 1816, temperatures were well below normal, with snow falling as late as early June. This was disastrous for farmers, who referred to it as 'the year without a summer' (**2.3**). It took several years for the dust to settle out from the atmosphere. The summers of 1817 and 1818 were not very good in New England either, leading many settlers to decide that they should give up trying to farm the difficult soils of the region and try their hand in the newly opening agricultural lands in the American Midwest.

**Figure 2.3** Average July temperatures in Toronto, Canada from 1780 to 1870, showing the unusually low temperatures in 1816 and 1817, which followed the explosive eruption of Tambora, Indonesia, in 1815

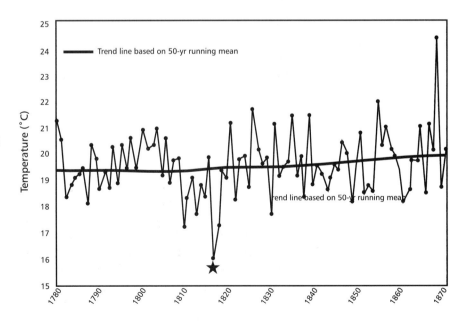

Similar stories of agricultural disruption are recorded in the history books of Europe and the Far East, where farmers commonly lived at a subsistence level and could not afford to miss a year of food production. There have been very few major volcanic eruptions in the past 50 years or so, but there is a lot of evidence that there were periods in the past when they were much more common. It is likely that such volcanic events would have had a significant impact on global climate at those times.

## The cryosphere

The cryosphere consists of mountain glaciers and continental ice sheets, seasonal snow and ice cover on land, as well as sea-ice. The high **albedo** (reflectivity) of snow- and ice-covered regions greatly affects global energy receipts. At present, about 8 per cent of the Earth's surface is permanently covered by snow and ice, mainly in Antarctica, Greenland and the Arctic Ocean, but this area fluctuates by 100 per cent on an annual basis due to the expansion of sea-ice and continental snow cover. The extent of snow and sea-ice in each hemisphere changes quite rapidly every year from winter to summer, but the area of glaciers and ice sheets changes only very slowly, on a time-scale of decades to centuries, or even longer for the slow-moving large polar ice sheets.

## The biosphere

This final component of the climate system consists of the plant and animal worlds and microbiota (for example, anaerobic bacteria in such things as rice paddies and cow guts). Vegetation affects:

■ The albedo of the Earth's surface.
■ The roughness of that surface and therefore wind speeds.
■ Evapotranspiration – that is, the amount and rate at which water leaves the ground.
■ Atmospheric composition, by removing carbon dioxide during photosynthesis, and at the same time producing oxygen. Also, where there is very little vegetation to cover the ground, dust particles (mainly silt) may be carried up into the air. On a large enough scale, dust in the air can affect the energy coming into the Earth from the Sun (or the energy radiated away from the Earth's surface). Today, deserts cover 18 per cent of the continents, so they are a significant source of dust, but during the last ice age the atmosphere was even dustier, because desert regions expanded (**2.4**). Even today, after rain in southern England has fallen on cars and evaporated, reddish deposits may be left. Often, this is Saharan dust, carried long distances from the African desert and washed out in the rainfall far from its original source.

People are, of course, part of the biosphere, and human activities play an increasingly important role in the climate system. Increases in atmospheric $CO_2$ concentrations, changes in natural vegetation, increases in dust particles entering the lower troposphere and reductions in atmospheric ozone concentrations in the stratosphere may all be attributed to worldwide human activities (see **Chapter 5**).

## Review

4 Explain why the geography of the Earth today has not always been the same as it is now.

5 What does the term **cryosphere** refer to?

6 Explain how explosive volcanic eruptions can affect global climate.

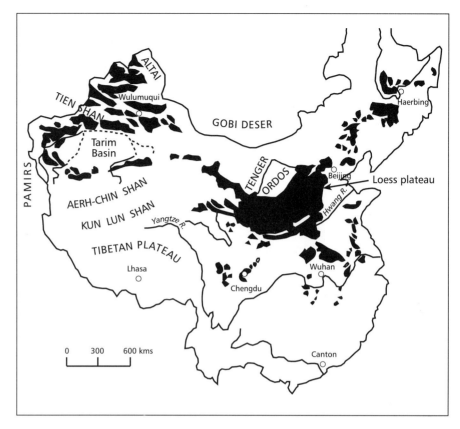

**Figure 2.4** During the ice ages, the world was much more arid than it is today and a great deal of wind-blown silt (known as **loess**) accumulated in some regions. These loess deposits (black areas on the map) are extremely thick in parts of China, burying the underlying landscape with deposits as much as 300 m thick in places. During wetter (interglacial) periods, soils formed on the loess only to be buried again beneath loess from subsequent glacial periods. Thus today you can see alternating layers of thick loess separated by thin interglacial soils

# Feedbacks in the system

All of the subsystems of the Earth's overall climate system are linked together in such a way that changes in one subsystem may lead to changes elsewhere (**2.1**). During ice ages, large ice sheets grew on the continents and, at high latitudes, extensive sea-ice covered the oceans. At the same time, deserts expanded and equatorial forests shrank. All of these changes resulted in a reduction in the amount of solar energy that was absorbed at the Earth's surface. This must have contributed further to the overall cooling that led to the ice ages in the first place (see **Chapter 4**). This type of change is referred to as **positive feedback**, because it reinforces the direction of change in which the system is already going (**2.5**).

At some point, other factors must have come into play to reverse this trend – otherwise, the ice sheets would have continued to grow in size, and would eventually have covered the entire planet (leading to a 'snowball Earth'). Such factors are referred to as **negative feedback** (**2.5**), because they would cause the system to change back to its original state. For example, if a cooler Earth resulted in less evaporation over the tropical oceans, there would be fewer clouds, less energy reflected back into outer space and more energy absorbed at the surface. This would then lead to warming of the oceans at low latitudes, which would set up a strong gradient in

**Figure 2.5** How feedbacks affect temperatures

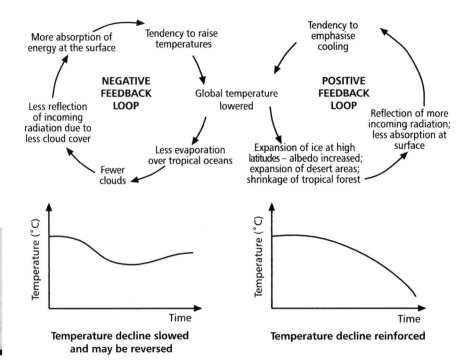

**Review**

7 Give an example of a positive feedback process that may occur in the global climate system.

temperature between the Equator and the Poles, and a strong ocean circulation that would carry warm water poleward. This, in turn, might help to melt the ice sheets and so lead to more energy being absorbed in those regions. In this case, the reduction in cloudiness would be considered as a negative feedback, counteracting the tendency for the Earth to cool off. Climate variations over time have resulted from changes in forcing factors and the relative balance of positive or negative feedbacks operating at various times.

## SECTION D

## The Earth's energy balance

Energy from the Sun (in the form of short-wave solar radiation) that reaches the outer extremities of the Earth first has to pass through the atmosphere. There are many processes that reduce the amount of energy that eventually reaches the surface (**2.6**). Gas molecules and particles (aerosols) scatter some of the energy back into space, while some 20 per cent of it is absorbed by certain atmospheric gases, such as ozone. Incoming solar radiation is also intercepted by clouds, that reflect a similar percentage of the energy back into space. Thus, only about half the energy that originally entered the outer atmosphere finally reaches the Earth's surface. This energy is then absorbed by the land surface, and in the upper layers of the ocean, and is re-radiated at longer wavelengths. The amount of energy absorbed depends on the reflectivity (**albedo**) of the surface. Bright surfaces (such as snow and ice) or sandy deserts reflect much of the incoming short-wave (solar) energy back to space, whereas darker surfaces

**Figure 2.6** The mean annual radiation and energy balance of the Earth

Of the 168 W m⁻² (watts per metre squared) absorbed by the Earth's surface, there is a net radiative loss of 66 W m⁻² (the net loss from long-wave emissions 390 W m⁻², less counter-radiation from the atmosphere to the surface 324 W m⁻). The balance of energy at the surface (the net radiation – i.e. 66 W m⁻² + 102 W m⁻²) is transferred by latent heat transfer (evaporation) and sensible heat transfer ('thermals' in this diagram).

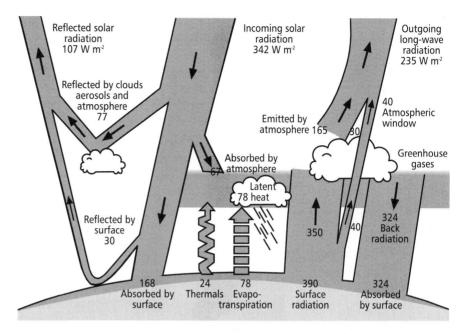

(such as forests or oceans) absorb more energy. So the distribution of the continents and the oceans, the extent of ice sheets and sea-ice, and the distribution of different vegetation types all affect the amount of energy absorbed at the Earth's surface, as well as the geographical pattern of energy absorption (**2.6**).

Long-wave radiation is absorbed by greenhouse gases, causing the lower atmosphere to warm. This in turn radiates energy, some to space and some back towards the surface, so there is a continual energy exchange back and forth. However, overall, the amount of energy entering the system equals the amount that is radiated away, so the system as a whole stays in balance. Part of the energy that was absorbed at the Earth's surface is not radiated away, but is transferred directly to the adjacent atmospheric layers as **sensible heat** (heat that you can feel). This direct warming of the lower atmosphere raises its temperature, so that the air in turn radiates more energy at longer wavelengths (some of which leaves the Earth towards space). Heat is also transferred from the Earth's surface via evaporation (**latent heat transfer**). This is especially important over the oceans, where water is 'energised' by the addition of solar energy, converting the liquid water to water vapour. Eventually, that water vapour may condense, often in a different region and at higher elevations. The latent heat that first caused the water to become a vapour will be released into the atmosphere, raising its temperature. In these ways, then, energy from the Sun cascades through the atmosphere and is transferred through many pathways, warming the Earth and the atmosphere before it is eventually lost back into space.

It is easy now to imagine how important many factors can be in causing climates to change over time, and to picture how a change in one variable can affect many others. If the energy emitted by the Sun changed, it would have a direct effect on all of the processes just described. Take the more specific case of an increase in cloudiness. To start with, this would affect the amount of energy that reaches the surface, in most cases causing temperatures to fall. This might lead to longer winters and more persistent snow cover, which could in turn reduce the amount of energy absorbed. Further cooling could cause sea-ice to expand geographically and, eventually, ice sheets to develop on land. A cooler ocean could absorb more carbon dioxide (because carbon dioxide is more soluble at lower temperatures), so this might lead to a reduction in the greenhouse effect and then to further cooling. No doubt feedback of this type has been important over geological time but, equally, there have probably been dozens of other more subtle factors that have operated to balance things out, and to bring the Earth back towards a more stable condition.

# Case study: Variations of the Rhône glacier over the past 400 years

The Rhône glacier is one of the ten largest in Switzerland, being 10 km in length and covering 17 square miles (44 km$^2$). However, this is nothing compared to its size during the last ice age. At that time, it was over 300 km long. Since the ice age it has been reduced in size as it has adjusted to new climatic circumstances, but this shrinkage has not been at an even rate. For example, during the Little Ice Age (1550–1850) it actually grew. The overall trend since 1600, however, has been of retreat. Since 1602, the volume has decreased by about 400 million cubic metres.

1  a  Measure in a straight line between points A (at the snout in 1602) and B (at the snout in 1969). Approximately how far did the glacier retreat between 1602 and 1969?

   b  Comment on the rate of retreat over the intervening years. Has retreat been even over the entire period?

   c  Suggest an explanation for your answer.

2  Use the long profile (2.8) to suggest by how much the Rhône glacier thinned during the period from 1602 to 1969.

3  Draw a sketch of the Rhône glacier in 1993 and annotate it to show the position of the ice in 1848. What physical features on the 1993 photograph show that ice was recently much more extensive than it is now? Label the features on your sketch.

4  Many hydroelectric power dams (such as the Grande Dixence Dam) have been constructed a few kilometres downstream from the present positions of alpine glaciers. From the point of view of climatic change, suggest why this might not, in the long run, be a particularly good idea.

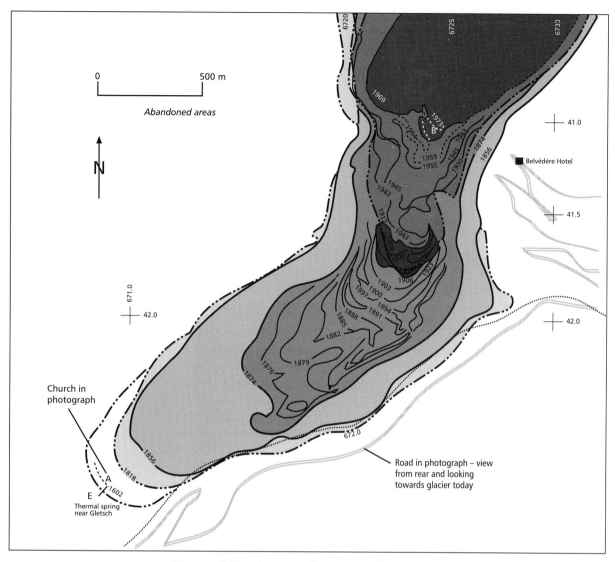

**Figure 2.7** Variations in the position of the terminus of the Rhône glacier since 1602

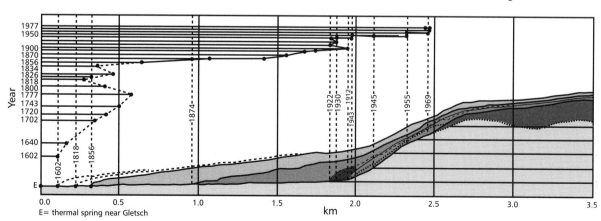

**Figure 2.8** A cross-section through the glacier, showing how it has changed in volume over time

**Figure 2.9** The retreat of the Rhône glacier, as shown by **(a)** a reconstruction of its extent in 1848 and **(b)** a photograph taken in 1993

We can imagine global climate as a system that has shifted back and forth between ice ages and warmer periods, as the relative importance of different factors has varied over time. Today, we are in a warm interglacial period; we have been so for about 11 000 years – more or less the period since agriculture was first 'invented'. If the factors that led to ice ages in the past are understood, it may become possible to predict that, thousands of years from now, the Earth will again be heading towards another ice age. But this is far enough away that it need not concern us. Of more immediate concern is the change in greenhouse gases over the past 150 years, and the climatic changes that are predicted for the next century. These changes will occur at a far greater rate than at any time that we know of in geological history, so it is very difficult to know what the effect will be on global climate. Computer models of the climate system (similar to weather forecasting models) are being used to try to understand these effects and to provide a reliable forecast of our climate in the future (see **Chapter 5**).

1 Study the two climographs for Plymouth, Massachusetts and Plymouth, England (**2.10**).

   **a** Describe the climates of the two places, remembering to make statements about each of the following:
- maximum temperature (and month)
- minimum temperature (and month)
- annual temperature range
- approximate total precipitation (add the values for the bars)
- seasonal distribution of precipitation

   **b** Write a short account that compares the climates of the two Plymouths.

   **c** Explain the similarities and differences in climate that you have identified in **b**.

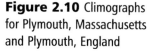

**Figure 2.10** Climographs for Plymouth, Massachusetts and Plymouth, England

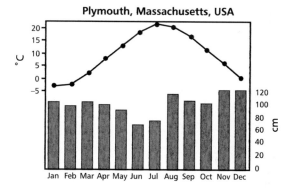

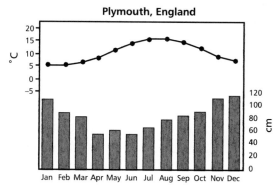

2 'Climatic change has been a normal state of affairs for the Earth over geological time.' Discuss.

3 Identify those factors that lead us to the conclusion that future climatic change may well occur at a hitherto unprecedented rate.

# Evidence of climatic change

## Introduction

The Earth's climate is constantly changing. These changes are due to many factors. Some of them lie outside the Earth system (external factors, such as changes in the energy from the Sun or in the Earth's position in relation to the Sun) and some of them are internal to the Earth system (such as the uplift of mountain chains, shifts in ocean currents and explosive volcanic eruptions). All of these causal factors are discussed in more detail in **Chapter 4**.

The important point to stress here is that changes occur on many different time-scales. On long (geological) time-scales, continents shift position due to plate tectonics; mountain ranges are created and worn down. These alter surface conditions and ocean currents, and lead to changes in the pattern of climate over the Earth's surface, even if the amount of energy from the Sun remains the same. Such long-term changes in climate are recorded in ocean sediments deposited during earlier geological epochs, although today those sediments may have been converted into solid rock and uplifted by immense pressures over the intervening years. Thus, we can find today, across all of southern England, sedimentary rocks (chalk, limestone and so on) containing fossils that record the environments of former seas. Study of these fossils provides information about water temperature and salinity in oceans that have long since disappeared. By examining rocks of similar age from around the world, geologists are able to build up a picture of the physical geography of the world at particular times in the past, including what the climate was like. Where possible, they also examine the evidence contained in old lake sediments and wind-blown (aeolian) material, as well as swamp deposits that may now be in the form of coal. All of these rocks help to establish the climates of ages past.

Because we cannot directly measure the parameters of past climates using the sorts of instruments with which we monitor today's weather, we have to infer those parameters from the types of evidence just described. These sources are known as **palaeoclimatic proxies**. Piecing together the evidence that they provide enables scientists to gain a rough picture of how global temperatures have changed over

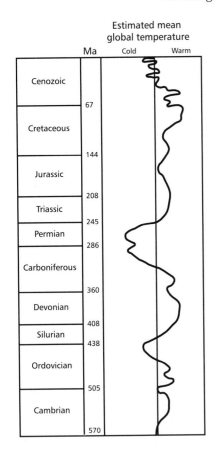

**Figure 3.1** A generalised temperature history of the Earth

The temperature history is plotted as related to the present global mean. Studying the proxy record of paleoclimate is rather like looking through a telescope held the wrong way around – for recent periods there is evidence of short-term climatic variations, but these cannot be resolved in earlier periods.

## Review

1 Look at **3.1**. Why do you think that the temperature changes are shown in more detail in recent times?

2 In your own words, define the term **palaeoclimatic proxies**.

millions of years. Figure **3.1** shows that the Earth has been generally warmer for much of the past 500 million years, and that in recent geological time (the late Cenozoic) there has been a series of cold oscillations – the ice ages.

The evidence that we have for the most recent changes in climate is still quite fresh and relatively unaltered, whereas our understanding of events during previous ice ages (for example, at the end of the Carboniferous and the beginning of the Permian periods, 250–300 million years ago) is very sketchy (**3.1**). Nevertheless, we can learn a lot about how the Earth system works, and what factors are important in maintaining a stable climate (or causing it to change), by studying the relatively recent past. For this reason, we will now focus on the most recent geological epoch, the Quaternary period.

**SECTION B**

# Climatic change during the Quaternary period

The Quaternary period spans the past 2 million years or so, and covers the period of time during which humans evolved from ape-like animals (*Homo erectus*) to modern human beings (*Homo sapiens*). Over this interval, the world has experienced strong oscillations in climate, from cold glacial periods (**ice ages**) to warm interglacials, such as the period that we are now in, which is known as the Holocene interglacial. During glacial times, vast ice sheets formed over large areas of the Northern Hemisphere continents.

## Case study: The ice-age world

In the most recent ice age, the Laurentide Ice Sheet covered much of North America, reaching a thickness of more than 2500 m over what is now Hudson's Bay (**3.2**). Similarly, a large ice sheet developed over Scandinavia and merged with a smaller one over Scotland. These ice sheets grew from water that evaporated from the oceans, condensing as snow over the continents. So much water (snow) became locked up in the ice sheets that the sea level fell by 120 m around the world, causing many regions that are today separated by water to become one continuous land mass. Thus, eastern Siberia and Alaska were linked, as today's Bering Strait was then exposed land and, similarly, the archipelago between the mainland of South-East Asia and Australia became an almost continuous land bridge (**3.3**). These land bridges were important migration routes for early humans, who are thought to have moved into Australia and North America during these periods of lower sea level. So, the ice-age world had a different coastline, and ice sheets extended like mountainous domes into the lower atmosphere.

In the oceans, sea-ice reached much lower latitudes (probably as far as the British Isles in the North Atlantic) and warm ocean currents that now

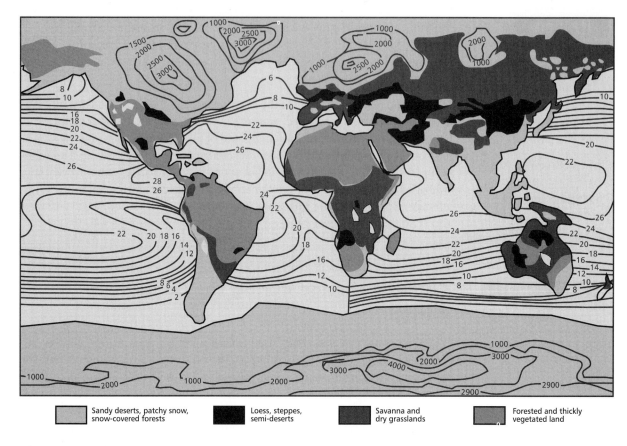

| | Sandy deserts, patchy snow, snow-covered forests | | Loess, steppes, semi-deserts | | Savanna and dry grasslands | | Forested and thickly vegetated land |

**Figure 3.2** A map of the ice-age world

During the last ice age, large ice sheets developed over North America and northwestern Europe, as well as in parts of Siberia. Smaller ice caps covered mountainous regions such as the Alps, the southern Andes and the southern Alps of New Zealand. The area of land with permafrost expanded and vegetation patterns around the world were altered due to lower temperatures, more arid conditions and a lower atmospheric carbon dioxide level.

extend to 70°N or more in the North Atlantic were further south, crossing the Atlantic towards Portugal. On the continents, large areas that are forested today became zones of arctic tundra, glaciers expanded to coalesce as ice sheets in alpine areas and forests were displaced to lower elevations. In the continental interiors of Asia and North America, conditions became quite dry, and wind-blown dust was extensive. In the Tropics, conditions were equally dry in many areas, and the equatorial forest zones contracted.

If we were able to see our planet as it was 25 000 years ago, we would be confronted by something quite unrecognisable, compared to what we see today. Since then, however, the ice sheets have mostly disappeared, leaving only Greenland and Antarctica covered by ice. The sea level has risen by 120 m, and vast areas of the Eurasian and North American continents, formerly buried under ice, are now covered by boreal forest. Sea-ice is mainly confined to the Arctic Ocean and the area around Antarctica, and rain forests cover much of the lowland Tropics. These dramatic environmental changes have gone on repeatedly during the Quaternary period. Over the past 2 million years, there have perhaps been more than 20 oscillations between glacial and interglacial conditions. But how do we know this?

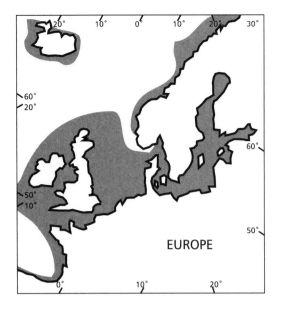

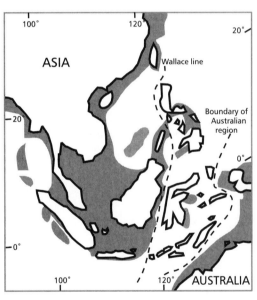

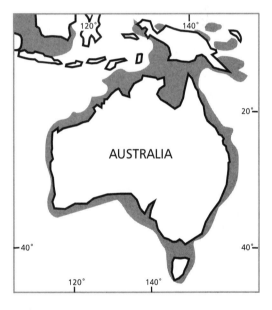

**Figure 3.3** As the continental ice sheets 'locked up' water from the oceans on land during the ice ages, the sea level fell by 120 m. This led to many areas that are now underwater becoming exposed as 'land bridges' (shaded on the maps) between continents

## Review

3 The extension of ice sheets and glaciers on the continents was one of a number of changes that occurred during the ice ages. Identify other changes.

# Evidence from the oceans and lakes

Water in the world ocean has a certain isotopic composition. Isotopes are variations in the atomic mass of an element. In the case of oxygen (which makes up part of the $H_2O$ molecule) there are two important isotopes, $^{18}O$ and $^{16}O$: $^{18}O$ is the heavier isotope, having more mass (two more neutrons) in its atomic nucleus. Water molecules may contain both isotopes, but when water evaporates, the molecules of water that contain the heavier isotope do not change from the liquid to the vapour state as easily as those that contain the lighter $^{16}O$ isotope.

## Foraminifera and the isotopic record

During ice ages, water is continuously being removed from the oceans and stored on land in the form of snow and ice, whereas during interglacials most of the water that falls on continents returns to the oceans through rivers. The result is that during glacial times, when water molecules are removed from the oceans by evaporation but not returned via condensation and rainfall, the remaining ocean water slowly becomes depleted in molecules with the lighter isotope (or, you could say, relatively enriched in water with the heavier isotope). In other words, the growth of ice sheets on land not only caused the sea level to fall, but it also changed the chemical (isotopic) composition of the entire world ocean. We know that this was so because of tiny organisms (a form of zooplankton known as **foraminifera**) that build a calcareous shell around themselves. They live in many parts of the ocean and the chemical composition of the shells that they construct is affected by the chemistry of the ocean waters in which they live.

**Figure 3.4** The oxygen isotope record that is typically obtained from the analysis of calcium carbonate in foraminifera from ocean sediments

Note that the convention is to present graphs like this, with the present to the left. Several of the following graphs follow this pattern.

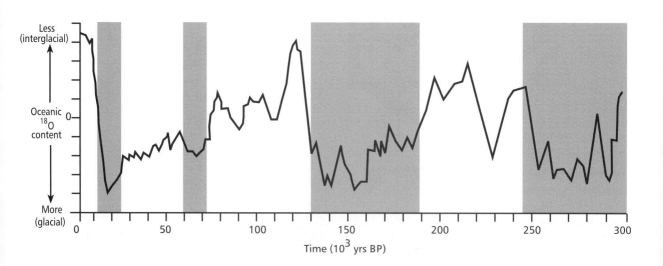

When ice sheets built up on the land during glacial periods, water molecules that eventually became stored on land as ice had slightly more of the lighter isotope ($^{16}O$) than the ocean water, so eventually the composition of the world ocean became slightly 'enriched' in the heavy isotope ($^{18}O$). The amount of water stored on land can be estimated by how much the ocean was enriched in the heavy isotope ('More' on the figure). In effect, this oxygen isotope record provides a record of past glaciations (and past sea-level changes), with the glacial periods shown here as shaded periods.

When foraminifera die, the hard shells fall to the ocean floor, to accumulate as ocean sediment. Cores of sediment recovered from the deep oceans provide a record of these organisms that goes back in time, as successive generations of shells have been deposited on those of their predecessors. By analysing the isotopic composition of the calcium carbonate in these shells, a picture of changing ocean chemistry over time (and hence of the growth and decay of ice sheets on the continents) can be constructed. Figure **3.4** shows how the world's climate shifted rapidly from a cold (glacial) period 190 000–130 000 years ago to a warmer (interglacial) climate 125 000 years ago, then slowly returned to a glacial maximum episode 20 000–25 000 years ago, followed by another rapid shift to the present interglacial climate, which began around 10 000 years ago.

## Pollen grains

The marine isotope record constructed from the chemistry of foraminifera shells only gives a 'big picture' view of the Earth's climate. It clearly shows the major shifts, as between glacial and interglacial periods, on a global scale. But it does not reveal how climates in particular parts of the world might have varied. For this, additional proxies are used. In addition to the examples mentioned in **Section A**, lake sediments may contain pollen grains that were deposited from the vegetation in the local region (**3.5**). Pollen grains are extremely resistant to decay and have a form that differs from one plant type to another. Cores of sediment from lakes can thus give a picture of what vegetation was like in the past. Since the distribution of vegetation is largely controlled by climate, an understanding of changes in the plant communities of an area over time can be used to infer how the climate in that particular location may have changed over time. Pollen grains, in lake sediments and in peat bogs, are thus palaeoclimate proxies.

**Figure 3.5** Pollen grains under the microscope. Each type of plant has a different shape of pollen and the grains embedded in geological deposits can be used to identify the vegetation (and therefore the general climatic conditions) that were present when the deposits were formed.

**Review**

**4** In your own words, explain how the evidence provided by foraminifera, pollen grains and diatoms helps us to reconstruct past climates.

## Diatoms

Another example of how past climate can be reconstructed is through the study of diatoms – tiny organisms that secrete a protective cover of silica. In some lakes, the type of diatoms present in the water is dependent on salinity. If salinity increases in a semi-arid environment, due to higher temperatures and/or less rainfall, the type of diatoms that thrive in the lake will change, and this will be recorded in the lake sediments when the organisms die and fall to the lake floor. Thus shifts in the species composition of diatoms over time, as revealed by the analysis of cores of lake sediments, can be used to identify changes in the hydrology of the lake. Those hydrological changes, in their turn, may be interpreted as the response to changes in the local climate. By studying such sediments in many locations, palaeoclimatologists are able to build up a picture of how climates have changed over large areas and long periods of time (**3.6**).

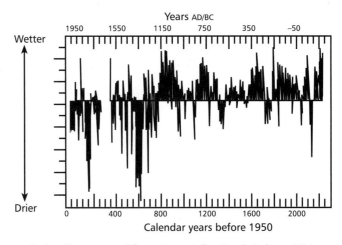

**Figure 3.6** The diatom record from Moon Lake, North Dakota, USA

In this closed-basin lake (which has no outlet), the relative amounts of evaporation and rainfall affect the salinity of the water, which in turn affects the type and number of diatoms that live in the water. By examining the diatoms in lake sediments, an estimate of water salinity can be made. The record indicates that before about AD 1200 the lake water was more saline, which suggests that this area was more arid for much of the past ~2200 years. Confirmation of this interpretation requires studies of other lakes in this region. Note the missing data for the period 1600–1700.

**SECTION D**

# Evidence-rich ice cores

A remarkably detailed record of past changes in climate has been established from ice cores, mainly from Antarctica, Greenland and high mountain ice-caps in the Tropics. In such locations, snow that accumulates at high elevations does not melt: it is buried by later snowfall and compressed into ice. As more snow accumulates, the ice itself is slowly compressed, flowing outwards towards the edge of the ice sheet. By drilling down through the centre of an ice sheet, a record of past snowfall events can be recovered. The longest record so far obtained is from Vostok in

Antarctica, and covers the past 420 000 years. In Greenland, ice cores provide a clear record of approximately the past 100 000 years (almost to the last interglacial), while in the Tropics, an ice core from a height of over 6000 m in Peru goes back over 25 000 years. In some areas, such as central Greenland, it is possible to identify annual layers in the ice, enabling a very detailed analysis to be made, almost year by year, over the past 40 000 years.

## Salt content

The ice from these cores contains an amazing amount of information about past climate. The snow itself contains minute traces of chemicals washed from the air through which it passed en route to the ice sheet. For example, variations in the amount of sodium ions ($Na^+$) in Greenland are thought to reflect changes in the extent of sea-ice. When there is a lot of open water nearby, the wind can pick up tiny salt crystals (sodium chloride), which may then be deposited on the snow. High levels of sodium ions in an ice core are interpreted as indicating periods with very little sea-ice.

## Dust content

Another example of how ice cores provide useful information about past climate can be seen in the very pronounced difference between ice from glacial and interglacial periods. During glacial times, the atmosphere was much dustier than today, due to a combination of higher wind speeds and drier conditions in the continental interiors. These periods show up in ice cores as much dirtier layers, as compared with the cleaner layers accumulated during interglacial periods. Dust from glacial times formed the extensive loess deposits in China (**2.4**) and other areas. In ice cores from Antarctica, the dust has been chemically identified as coming mainly from Patagonia (Argentina), which was even drier at that time than it is today.

## Isotopic composition

In ice cores, the snow itself also provides an indirect record of the temperature when it formed. The relative amounts of the two isotopes, $^{16}O$ and $^{18}O$, contained in the frozen water provide a sort of 'palaeo-thermometer' of temperature readings. Basically, the higher the ratio of $^{16}O$ to $^{18}O$ isotopes, the colder the air temperature was when the snow was first precipitated from clouds. Studies have also shown that exactly the same process occurs in the hydrogen isotopes of water. Hydrogen has two stable isotopes ($^1H$ and $^2H$) and these behave in the same way, with the ratio between them increasing in favour of the lighter isotope ($^1H$) as temperatures fall.

# Case study: The isotope record from an Antarctic ice core

**Figure 3.7** The record of hydrogen isotopes (deuterium) in water molecules from an ice core from Vostok, Antarctica, over the past 420 000 years. This shows cycles of glaciations, during which values were low, and interglacials (such as the present one, which began about 10 000 years ago), during which values were higher

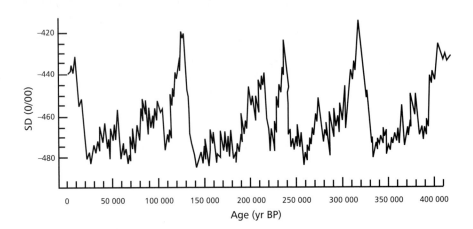

Figure **3.7** shows the hydrogen isotope record of an ice core taken from the Antarctic ice-cap. It covers a period of 420 000 years. Just as with the isotope record from foraminifera in ocean sediments (**3.4**), there is evidence of a fairly regular series of glacials and interglacials, as well as intervening, relatively warm periods known as **interstadials**. Each 'cycle' lasted about 100 000 years as temperatures slowly declined towards the coldest part of the glacial period, followed by an abrupt warming (known as a **termination**). Termination 1 occurred between 18 000 and 12 000 years ago. During that time, temperatures in the polar regions increased rapidly. The continental ice sheets melted very quickly, returning the water that had accumulated on the continents back into the oceans and bringing the isotopic composition of that water back to interglacial levels.

Ice cores from Greenland reveal a remarkable feature of the last ice age (**3.8**). Isotope values in snow from that time underwent very dramatic rapid changes – from almost glacial levels to almost interglacial levels over periods as short as a few decades. Similar abrupt changes in climate can be seen in Antarctic ice cores, but they are less dramatic than in the case of Greenland. Rapid climatic changes have also been identified in lake sediment records from as far apart as the Mediterranean region and China. Possible reasons for these sudden changes are explored in **Chapter 4**.

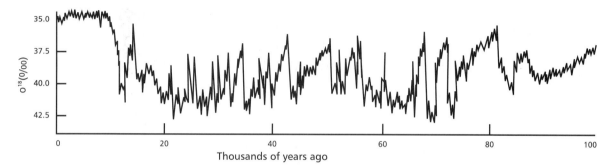

Figure 3.8 The record of oxygen isotopes in water molecules from an ice core through the Greenland Ice Sheet. Rapid changes between cold and warmer periods occurred frequently during the last ice age, apparently as a result of changes in the circulation of the North Atlantic Ocean (see the case study on page 25)

## Greenhouse gases

Ice-core records are also important because bubbles of air that were trapped in the ice as it became compressed provide tiny 'time capsules' of the atmosphere over time. They can be used to reconstruct how the composition of the atmosphere has changed from glacial to interglacial periods. Of most significance is the record of important greenhouse gases – carbon dioxide ($CO_2$) and methane ($CH_4$) – which have now been traced over the past 420 000 years.

The amounts of the gases varied significantly, from low levels during glacial times to high levels during interglacials. But the remarkable thing is that they reached more or less the same low levels in all of the past four glacial periods, and the same higher levels in the past few interglacials. This suggests that there have been processes operating on Earth that tend to

Figure 3.9 The record of two important greenhouse gases – $CO_2$ and $CH_4$ – in air bubbles that were trapped in an ice core from Vostok, Antarctica. During glacial times, greenhouse gas levels fell to low levels, but they rapidly increased during interglacial periods. Today, due to human activity, the levels of these gases are far higher than at any time in the past 420 000 years (see also **5.3**)

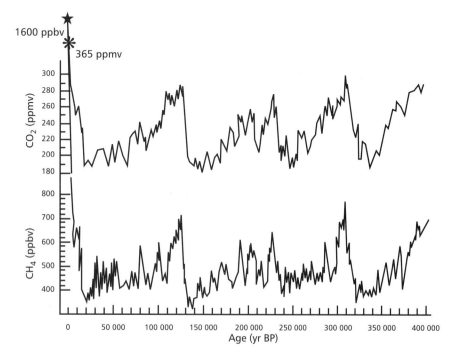

**Review**

5 Explain and exemplify what is meant by the term **palaeoclimatic proxies**.

6 Check that you understand the importance of ice cores as sources of evidence about climatic change.

keep the world within certain limits. As we saw in **Chapter 2**, when things shift towards a glacial condition, processes begin to operate that prevent the world from drifting too far in one direction – in other words, from becoming either completely glaciated or one vast hot desert.

To some scientists, this suggests that planet Earth functions as a living organism, balancing its own environment to help maintain habitable conditions. This is the basis for the so-called **Gaia hypothesis** (Gaia was the Greek goddess of Earth). Others, however, explain the phenomenon as simply the inevitable result of interacting forces that tend to compensate for each other.

Just why the changes in the $CO_2$ and $CH_4$ levels took place is complicated. What we can be more certain about is that variations in the levels of these greenhouse gases no doubt contributed to the climatic changes that took place during the Quaternary period, but that they were secondary factors. The primary driving forces behind the glacial–interglacial cycles were changes in the Earth's orbit relative to the Sun (see **Chapter 4**). However, it is worth noting that, mainly as a result of the rate at which the burning of fossil fuels has increased over the past 100 years, the $CO_2$ level has now risen to 360 parts per million by volume (ppmv). This is far beyond the record for any time in the past 420 000 years (**3.9**). The same is true for the $CH_4$ level. Furthermore, these record levels have been reached very rapidly, so that the Earth and its biosphere have had virtually no time to adjust (see **Chapter 5**).

## Some other sources

There are many sources of evidence about past climates other than those already discussed. For example, written evidence can provide a wealth of information. Because the weather was so important to sailors, they kept weather records in great detail during their voyages. The whaling logs of the 19th century are particularly invaluable documents. They give us a good idea of prevailing wind directions and the extent of sea-ice in the northern seas. Records from Spanish galleons sailing between Acapulco (Mexico) and Manila (in the Philippines) in the 17th century reveal the strength of winds in the equatorial Pacific, and hence provide information about El Niño conditions in the distant past (see page 47).

On a broader front, **phenology** (the study of the timing of recurrent biological phenomena) investigates factors such as the dates when trees burst into leaf or blossom, when crops are harvested and when birds and other animals migrate. Events such as these are indications of seasonal patterns, which may themselves have changed over time. Written records about past weather conditions in China, Japan and Europe extend back many centuries. These provide valuable information about the frequency of extreme weather events, and in some cases have enabled past weather patterns (pressure maps) to be reconstructed.

Tree rings also provide a continuous record of climate. **Dendroclimatology** (the study of climate from tree rings) relies on the fact that many trees put on an annual growth layer that varies in width, in part due to seasonal and annual variations in weather and climate. In the case of the bristlecone pines of the western USA, the tree-ring record of past climates can cover a period of over 1000 years. To go further back in time, sub-fossil wood found in lakes and peat bogs (such as the bog oaks of the Fylde in Lancashire) is used to provide a record of climate that may extend even to glacial times.

Recent geological deposits, such as moraines, outwash materials and alluvium, can be used to date the advances and retreats of glaciers. Fossils, particularly of plants and insects in bogs and lake sediments can also be analysed to provide indications of past climates.

## Review

7 Explain how tree rings provide evidence of climatic change.

8 Can you discover any other sources of evidence about climatic change?

9 Why do we need to understand past climates as we try to anticipate how climate will change in the future?

**Figure 3.10** Varves (seasonal deposits) in lake sediments also reflect climate

During the summer, if there was a lot of water activity, from ice melt or heavy rainfall, then a lot of coarse material would be spread across the lake floor. When the lake became frozen in the winter, the remaining sediment would settle out. These processes can be observed in many northern areas (such as northern Canada) today, and comparisons between present formations and past deposits can assist in paleoclimate reconstruction.

## Enquiry

Refer to **3.3**. Find out the significance of the Wallace line and suggest how it relates to 'land bridges'.

# Natural causes of climatic change

So far, we have seen that climate varies on a wide range of time-scales, from long-term changes over geological periods to shorter variations over spans of a century or less. Because of this, it is not surprising to find that the causes of climatic change are also many and varied. Some of these causes (**forcing factors**) operate very slowly and their effects only become evident over time-scales of hundreds of thousands of years. Other forcing factors operate much faster and the changes that they bring about are superimposed on the longer-term variations. The climatic record examined in **Chapter 3** suggested that, in the long run, the Earth is heading into another ice age. Paradoxically, the world has just experienced the warmest decade for over 100 years (perhaps even 1000 years). Is this merely a short-term blip in a long-term decline? Or has human interference with the climate system propelled us into a new climate situation, unlike anything experienced in the past?

**SECTION A**

## Important forcing factors on geological time-scales

When we are investigating how the Earth's climate has changed over long periods of geological time, it is not possible to do so without understanding how the geography of the planet has also changed, particularly as a result of plate tectonics. Continents have been constantly on the move, rearranging the distribution of land masses relative to the Equator and the Earth's rotational axis (the North and South Poles).

### Case study: World geography through time

Today, Antarctica is centred over the South Pole, providing a land mass on which snow and ice have accumulated, to reach a thickness of over 4000 m in places. This high ice plateau is very reflective and causes the Earth to absorb far less incoming solar radiation in the Southern Hemisphere than it would otherwise. The land mass that we now call Antarctica was part of Gondwana (a 'super-continent' that also included the land masses that now make up South America, Africa, India, Australia and Antarctica) when it drifted over the South Pole, probably in

## Late Jurassic, 152 Million years ago

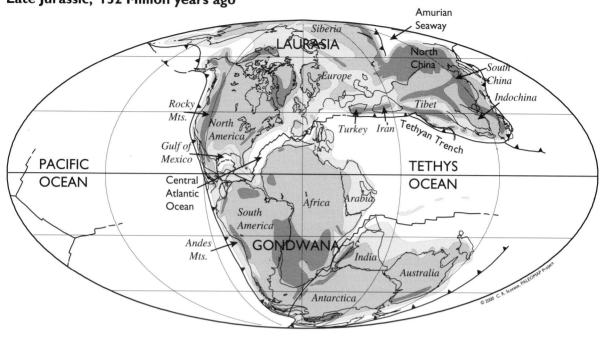

## Modern world

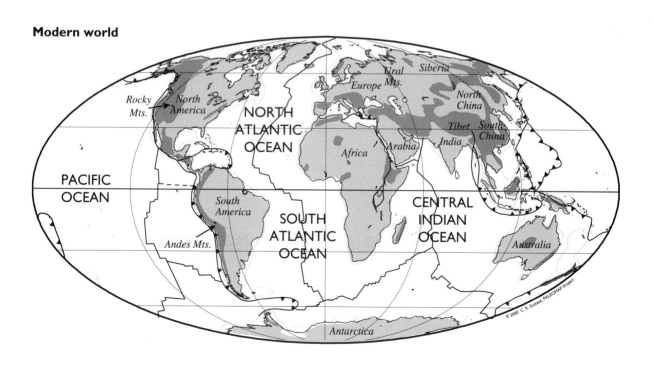

**250 million years in the future**

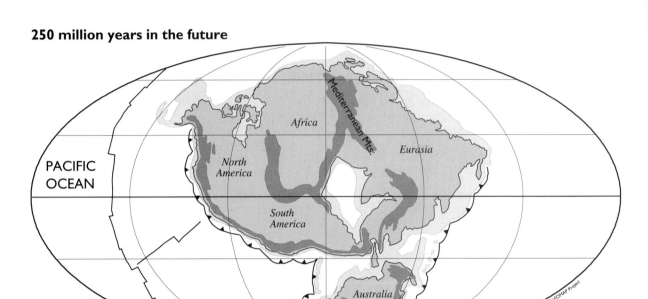

**Figure 4.1** The Earth's continental plates have drifted across the planet's surface throughout geological time, sometimes crashing into each other and pushing up material to form mountain ranges. Here we see the positions of the continents 152 million years ago, compared to the present and to what we can expect the world to look like 250 million years into the future

the Late Carboniferous or Permian (~300–280 million years ago). Prior to that time, it was not covered with snow and ice. The ice sheets appear to have developed as the continent continued to drift towards its polar position, but the surrounding land masses broke apart and drifted away from Antarctica, leaving it in the polar position of today. This poleward movement contributed greatly to the cooling of the planet during Cenozoic times (**3.1**). Other land masses have also shifted across the face of the planet. The extensive coal deposits of the Appalachians in North America, of central China and of southern Scotland and the North of England all testify to these areas having been in tropical locations during the Carboniferous period, because coal developed from tropical swamp deposits.

These changes in continental positions were accompanied by tectonic changes – mountain-building episodes when one plate pushed against another, causing rocks to be thrust far above sea level. Today, in the Swiss Alps, the contorted sediments of a former ocean basin can be seen towering above the peaceful valleys, a testimony to the awesome forces that have changed the face of the Earth over and over again on geological time-scales. Mountain ranges and continental ice sheets were not the only features of a changing global geography. Ocean basins have been created and then closed up, disrupting ocean currents and deep-water circulation.

For most of geological time (the Earth is now thought to date from over 4000 million years ago), we have only the vaguest idea of the changes that took place. But, clearly, the constant rearrangement of the Earth's geography led to climatic changes, as continents shifted from equatorial latitudes to the poles and vice versa. Only in the past few million years has the geography of the Earth become more or less as we see it today (although, of course, it is still changing at a very slow rate). Modern methods of accurate measurement, such as global positioning systems (GPS), show that some plates are still drifting apart, while others are approaching each other, and the occasional major volcanic eruption reminds us of the mobile magma chambers that lurk beneath the Earth's surface.

---

While these geological forces have been operating on the Earth, the Sun has also slowly changed, which has led to long-term variations in its energy output. Solar physicists calculate that the Sun's brightness (its **luminosity**) has increased by as much as 30 per cent over the past 4.7 billion years. This might suggest that, in its early days, the Earth experienced a much cooler climate in all locations. However, the geological evidence suggests that this was not so. Indeed, the Earth's temperature as a whole seems to be considerably lower now than it was 3 billion years ago. Why this is so remains unexplained, and is referred to as the 'faint young sun paradox'.

Several hypotheses have been put forward to explain the paradox. One idea is that the Earth's early atmosphere contained much higher levels of greenhouse gases, so that even though the Sun emitted far less energy, the Earth was able to retain more of the long-wave radiation emitted from the planet's surface than it does today. Another suggestion is that the oceans were less restricted by the continents. The continents were perhaps more separated than they are today, so that the warm equatorial waters were able to carry heat to higher latitudes more easily, thereby maintaining a moderately warm Earth as a whole.

More research is needed before we can be sure of exactly why the Earth used to be warmer than is predicted by theory, but one other factor must surely be considered. As plant life developed on Earth, it used carbon dioxide as a basic building block to produce carbohydrates (plant tissue) through the process of photosynthesis. This must have slowly led to the extraction of carbon dioxide from the atmosphere, reducing the greenhouse effect (**2.2**). As the plants died, together with the animals that ate them, their tissues became 'locked away' in sediments that ultimately became rocks. Thus there may have been a slow reduction in atmospheric carbon dioxide levels as a result of life itself, and this may help to account for the long-term cooling of the Earth, at least for the period since life began to develop.

Ironically, since the Industrial Revolution, the burning of these now fossilised hydrocarbon deposits (the so-called **fossil fuels**, such as coal and oil) has meant putting back into the atmosphere the greenhouse gases that were removed long ago. Given the rate at which modern society has consumed fossil fuels, it is not too surprising that the concentration of carbon dioxide in the atmosphere has risen. Within less than a century, it has risen to a level not seen for hundreds of thousands – and quite probably millions – of years. Certainly, if the consumption of fossil fuels continues at the current rate, before the end of the 21st century $CO_2$ concentrations will exceed anything that the Earth has experienced for tens of millions of years. Needless to say, this is a matter that causes many people to view the future with great concern.

## Review

**1** How might you explain the fact that the Earth is now colder than it was 3 billion years ago, in spite of the fact that the Sun is now emitting more energy?

**2** Explain the links between plate tectonics and global climatic change.

SECTION B

# The Milankovich hypothesis

Throughout the past 2 million years, the climate of the Earth has been shifting back and forth between glacial and interglacial periods. It is now known that these changes have been driven (forced) by small changes in the position and orientation of the Earth in relation to the Sun. A careful explanation of the links between variations in the Earth's orbit due to the gravitational effects of the Sun, the Moon and other planets was first given by a Serbian engineer, Milutin Milankovich, in the 1920s.

Milankovich calculated that there have been three very important and fairly regular variations in the Earth's orbit, each with a different cycle length (period). To understand this, it must first be remembered that the Earth rotates on its axis (one rotation defines a day) and that as it rotates it

**Figure 4.2** The Earth's orbital configuration

The Earth revolves around the sun once per year. The orbit varies slightly, from circular to slightly elliptical (see **4.3**), which is termed the 'eccentricity'. The imaginary surface across which the Earth moves is the 'plane of the ecliptic'. The Northern Hemisphere winter results from the Earth being tilted on its axis, which orientates that hemisphere away from the Sun between the autumnal and spring equinoxes.

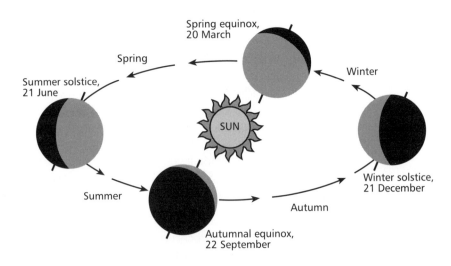

Spring equinox, 20 March

Spring

Summer solstice, 21 June

Winter

SUN

Winter solstice, 21 December

Summer

Autumn

Autumnal equinox, 22 September

moves around the Sun (one revolution approximately defines a year) (**4.2**). The Earth's orbit around the Sun is not exactly circular. It follows a slightly elliptical path, which means it is closest to the Sun at one part of its annual cycle, and furthest away at another. The axis of the Earth's rotation is not perpendicular; rather, it is tilted at about 23°. It is this tilt that determines day length and the seasons as the Earth passes around the Sun. The Northern Hemisphere tilts towards the Sun during the northern summer and away from it during the northern winter. The opposite applies to the Southern Hemisphere.

However, this angle of tilt (the **obliquity**) has not always been the same. It has varied slightly, from 21.8° to 24.4°, and this affects the maximum latitude at which the Sun is overhead in summer (the Tropics of Cancer and Capricorn are currently at 23.5°N and 23.5°S) as well as the latitude beyond which it remains dark all day for a good part of the winter (the Arctic and Antarctic Circles, currently at 66.5°N and 66.5°S). This oscillation in the angle of tilt varies regularly, with a period (cycle length) of about 41 000 years. These changes in obliquity have relatively little effect on the amount of energy received from the Sun at low latitudes, but they have a stronger influence at higher latitudes.

At the same time as the Earth's angle of tilt has varied, the time of year at which it is closest to the Sun has also changed (**4.3**). This is the result of a slight wobble in the Earth's rotation as it moves around the Sun, just as a spinning top might wobble on its axis. Today, the Earth is closest to the Sun

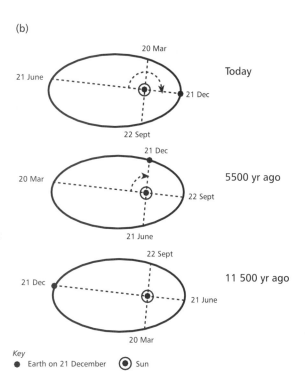

**Figure 4.3** The Earth's wobble and the timing of solstices

The Earth wobbles slightly on its axis, due to the gravitational pull of the Sun and Moon on the Earth (**a**). In effect, the axis moves slowly around a circular path and completes one revolution every 23 000 years, an effect known as 'precession of the equinoxes'. This results in the positions of the equinoxes (20 March and 22 September) and the solstices (21 June and 21 December) changing slowly around the Earth's orbit, with a period of ~23 000 years (**b**). Thus ~11 000 years ago the Earth was at perihelion (closest to the Sun on its annual orbit) at the time of the summer solstice, whereas today the summer solstice coincides with aphelion (furthest from the Sun on its annual orbit). The effect is independent of changes in the angle of tilt (obliquity) of the Earth, which varies with a period of ~41 000 years.

(a time called **perihelion**) in early January, and furthest away (**aphelion**) in early July. The Earth receives about 3.5 per cent more solar radiation at perihelion than at aphelion, so you might expect the Northern Hemisphere January temperatures to reflect that. However, as has been pointed out, the Northern Hemisphere is tilted away from the Sun at the time of year when perihelion occurs, so it barely benefits from this extra energy. On the other hand, the Southern Hemisphere is tilted towards the Sun at that time (long day lengths), so it does receive more energy. But because the Southern Hemisphere is mostly covered by a deep ocean, it does not actually heat up very much.

About 11 500 years ago, this situation was very different – the exact timing at which the Earth reaches perihelion (its closest position to the Sun) has not stayed the same. It has shifted slightly each year, with a period (cycle length) of about 21 000 years. Therefore, 11 500 years ago, it was closest to the Sun in July and furthest away in January. This resulted in perihelion coinciding with Northern Hemisphere's summer. At this time, summers were relatively warm, because the 'extra' solar radiation enabled the large continental land mass to heat up – more than the Southern Hemisphere's oceans were able to do when perihelion coincided with the southern summer.

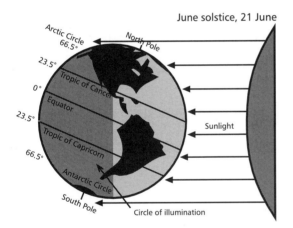

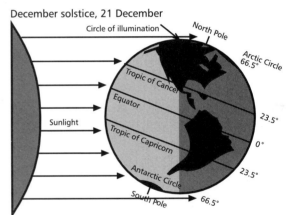

**Figure 4.4** The orbital effects on solar radiation reaching the Earth, and their time-scales

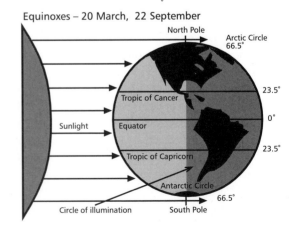

Because the Earth is tilted on its axis, as it revolves around the Sun the area in shadow (delimited by the 'circle of illumination') passes across different parts of the Earth. During the equinoxes, the circle goes right through the poles, so as the Earth rotates on its axis all locations experience 12 hours of darkness and 12 hours of light. During the Northern Hemisphere summer (June solstice), the tilt orientates the northern latitudes towards the Sun, so as the Earth rotates the period of daylight is longer than the period of darkness, and latitudes northward of the Arctic Circle experience daylight for all 24 hours. The opposite is true at the December (winter) solstice.

This variation over approximately 21 000 year cycles is called the **precession** of the equinoxes, because the position of the Earth on its orbit around the Sun has slowly shifted relative to the timings of the equinoxes. The equinoxes (21 March and 21 September) are when all places on Earth have 12 hours of darkness and 12 hours of light. This happens because the boundary between the part of the Earth that is illuminated by the Sun and the part that is in darkness passes right through both poles (**4.4**).

The final variation that Milankovich calculated is related to the orbit of the Earth around the Sun. Today, that orbit is not quite circular, but there have been times in the past when it has been almost exactly circular. Equally, there have been times when it has been even more elliptical. These variations are known as changes in the **eccentricity** of the Earth, with an irregular rhythm, or cycle, of around 100 000 years.

The effects of eccentricity variations and changes in the precession of the equinoxes are strongly linked. When the orbit was almost circular, there would have been virtually no difference in the solar radiation receipts at any time during the Earth's trip around the Sun (that is, perihelion and aphelion would be virtually indistinguishable). But when the Earth's orbital path was very elliptical, the difference in the radiation receipts at

**Figure 4.5** Changes in the eccentricity of the Earth's path around the Sun, the Earth's obliquity and the precession of the equinoxes (see also **4.3**), together with their combined effects

The eccentricity changes from an almost circular path to a more elliptical one (for example, 200 000 years ago). The obliquity, the tilt on the Earth's axis, is currently around 23.5°.

The eccentricity changes have a periodicity of about 90 000–100 000 years, the obliquity changes with a cycle of ~41 000 years and precession changes with a cycle of ~23 000 years.

Together, these effects combine to alter the distribution of solar energy, both geographically (from north to south) and from one month to the next. This is illustrated for three latitudes in the lower diagram, for the past 250 000 years.

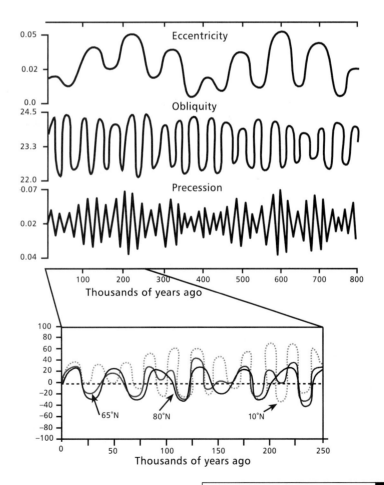

**3** Explain why:

- on 21 September, all places on Earth have equal hours of daylight and darkness
- on 21 December, places north of the Arctic Circle are in darkness for 24 hours
- in the UK, the days are much longer in the summer than in the winter.

**4** With the aid of a sketch diagram, try to summarise the essence of the Milankovich hypothesis.

perihelion and aphelion could have been quite large – in fact, as much as 30 per cent larger. This would have made a big difference between the seasons in the two hemispheres, depending on whether perihelion coincided with the northern or southern summer at those times.

Milankovich argued that these three variations – in obliquity, precession and eccentricity – must have changed the pattern of energy received by all places on the Earth from one year to the next. He showed that the overall energy received by the Earth hardly changed at all, but that there was a redistribution of the energy geographically (north to south) as well as seasonally, and that these changes were continuous from year to year. He then went on to suggest that the changes in solar energy at certain critical latitudes (around 60°N) during the Quaternary period were largely responsible for the growth and decay of the ice sheets in those regions. In other words, he felt that orbital forcing was the main factor that caused the ice ages.

Milankovich's work lay essentially forgotten until the 1970s, when a group of geologists who were studying marine sediments from the bottom of the ocean discovered that there had been regular changes in ocean temperature and ocean chemistry over time (see **Chapter 3**), and that these changes corresponded to the cycles that Milankovich had calculated. Today, there is a lot more evidence – from both the continents and the oceans – that the ice ages were driven by the subtle orbital changes that Milankovich highlighted. Even so, there are lots of questions that still have to be answered. For one thing, the changes in solar radiation due to variations in eccentricity are quite small, and seemingly not enough to cause the main 100 000 year cycle of the ice ages.

**SECTION C**

# Other possible causes

There must have been additional factors, most likely within the climate system itself, that built on or amplified the small solar energy changes that resulted from orbital variations. One possibility is that orbital changes led to changes in oceanic circulation that, in turn, caused changes in carbon dioxide concentrations in the atmosphere. During the ice ages, we know that $CO_2$ levels were low, and perhaps the drop in levels (and the reduction in the greenhouse effect) helped to cool the Earth. As colder conditions set in, the increase in sea-ice and snow cover would have reflected more incoming solar radiation and so, collectively, these things may have joined forces to bring about the growth of ice sheets on the continents.

Then, of course, there is the question of why the ice ages came to an end. The ocean sediments and ice cores show that the ice ages ended much more rapidly than they began. The view that scientists favour at the moment is that the large ice sheets on land grew to such a size that they became unstable. This, together with an increase in incoming solar radiation during summers at high latitudes due to orbital forcing, caused

**5** Explain the link between levels of $CO_2$ and climatic change.

the ice to melt in place or to drain away into the ocean through large fast-moving streams of ice. Millions of icebergs poured into the oceans in relatively short periods of time. In this way, the world has witnessed perhaps more than 20 glacials and interglacials over the past few million years. In fact, we know that the 'normal' (most common) condition of the Earth during the Quaternary period is not an interglacial, like the one we enjoy now, but a glacial period. Interglacials have been quite short, generally lasting for less than 10 000 years. This means that the present interglacial (called the Holocene) is due to end fairly soon in geological terms, perhaps within the next few thousand years. If no other factors come into operation, another glaciation may be expected. However, in the short term of the next century or so, human effects are likely to overwhelm the natural factors that cause climates to change.

**SECTION D**

## Internal variations

Milankovich's ideas certainly seem to explain most of the evidence for the timing of glaciations and interglacials, but the way in which the Earth reacts to variations in solar radiation remains uncertain. Just how the ice sheets developed, and how they collapsed, is more difficult to figure out. But we can be sure that interactions between the oceans, the snow and ice on land and sea, the atmosphere and the biosphere were all involved to some extent. Changes in the circulation patterns of the North Atlantic and the Pacific are good examples of climatic change brought about by internal feedbacks within the climate system.

### Case study: The thermohaline circulation

Ice-core records from Greenland (**3.8**) first revealed evidence that there were very abrupt changes in the climate of the North Atlantic region during the last ice age. Marine sediments also point to very sudden changes in the circulation of the Atlantic Ocean. These layers record periods when icebergs from collapsing ice sheets around the North Atlantic carried glacial sediments from the continental interiors to the oceans.

All of this has led to the hypothesis that these changes may be linked with times when the thermohaline circulation of the North Atlantic has changed.

Today, warm and relatively salty Gulf Stream water is carried northwards from the east coast of the USA towards the British Isles and Norway, bringing quite mild temperatures to western Europe (**4.6**). As the water cools, its density increases and the water sinks, to become what is termed **North Atlantic deepwater**. This dense water drifts slowly down

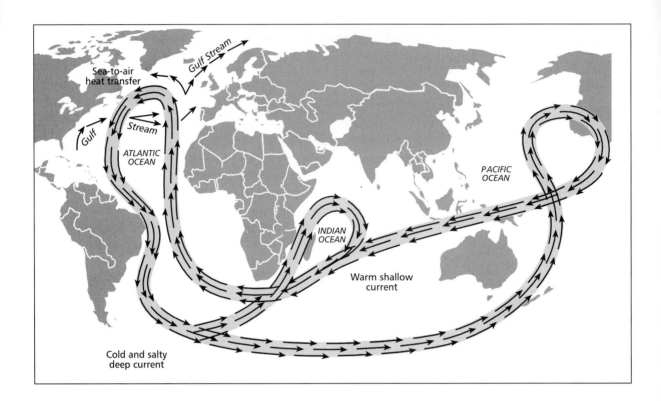

**Figure 4.6** The great ocean conveyor belt

to the ocean deeps and slowly circulates through to the Pacific. Eventually, it returns to the Atlantic via the Indian Ocean and around the tip of South America.

During the last ice age, it appears that there were times when this system either came to a complete halt or, at least, slowed right down. When this happened, it led to temperatures falling dramatically in Western Europe (because the warm waters of the Gulf Stream were reduced) but there were associated climatic effects all around the world. These sudden shifts in ocean circulation were the result of pulses of fresh water being discharged into the North Atlantic by collapsing ice sheets, which then reduced the surface water salinity (and therefore its density) disrupting the sinking process and the formation of deepwater (see **Section 5.4**).

A good example of an internal variation that operates today is the cycle of El Niño and La Niña events in the Pacific Ocean. Every few years, there is a shift in the temperature structure of the upper ocean. This is associated with changes in wind speed and direction, and with cloudiness and rainfall patterns over a vast area of the tropical Pacific. During El Niño episodes, warm waters occur in the eastern Pacific, together with heavy rainfall along the coast of Ecuador and parts of Peru. At the same time, the western Pacific, even as far west as Indonesia, becomes very dry. In effect, there has been a shift in the main rainfall belt towards the east.

**Figure 4.7** A comparison of El Niño events and normal atmospheric circulation

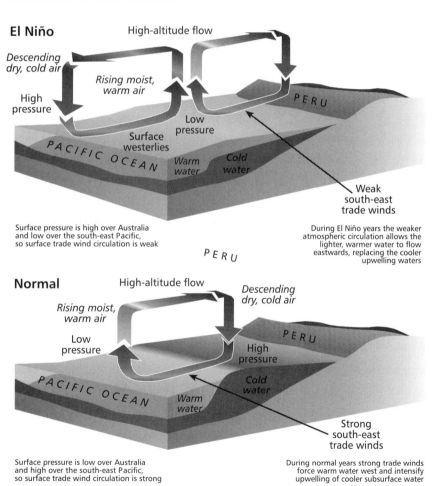

During La Niña episodes, the opposite condition prevails, with dry cool conditions off the coast of tropical South America, but much wetter conditions in the western Pacific. The atmospheric pressure oscillation

6 Summarise the causes and consequences of an El Niño event.

7 What feedbacks might operate to accentuate the effects of a volcanic event on the temperature of the Earth?

that goes along with the ocean circulation change is called the southern oscillation. Together, they go by the term **ENSO** (El Niño–Southern Oscillation). The overall changes involve such a large part of the globe that they then interact with the ocean and atmospheric circulation in other regions, setting up linkages (or teleconnections) that enable weather forecasters to predict what overall conditions are likely to occur during El Niño or La Niña episodes. However, not all El Niños are exactly the same, so the teleconnections are often unreliable predictors – except in a few locations such as the southern and southeastern USA, which is nearly always wet during El Niños and dry during La Niñas. See the website:

http://www.pmel.noaa.gov/toga-tao/el-nino/impacts.html

The ENSO is a good example of a variation in the climate system that is driven by internal processes, rather than being caused by something outside the Earth. Because there are abundant observations from the land, oceans and satellites, scientists have become very familiar with this cycle, and know that it generally switches back and forth over a period of 4–7 years. There may be other cycles that stretch over longer periods – perhaps over decades or centuries – that we do not yet fully recognise. For example, some have argued that there is a cycle in the North Atlantic of about 1500 years, with cold conditions recurring at this interval. Whether this cycle is due to an internal variation in the climate system or the result of some outside influence remains to be worked out. See also the website:

http://www.elnino.noaa.gov/

## Summing up

Finally, it is worth noting that not all climatic variations are regular; some may occur at very irregular intervals. For example, massive explosive volcanic eruptions – see the case study on page 15 – may send millions of tons of pulverised rock fragments into the upper atmosphere. The resulting 'dust veil' may block some of the incoming solar radiation, leading to cooling near the surface. Generally, the cooling only lasts for a few years – perhaps a decade at the most – but, in exceptional cases, it might set up the right conditions (such as more persistent snow cover, which reflects more sunshine) so that the cooling, once started, might last for a period long after the volcanic dust has settled from the atmosphere.

When we look back at the long-term history of the Earth, as recorded in sediments and other natural archives (see **Chapter 3**), it is important to understand that many of the factors discussed in this chapter must have been going on continuously, so that short-term oscillations in climate would have been taking place while slower long-term changes were also occurring. On the longest time-scale of tens if not hundreds of millions of years, the dominant forcing factors would have been changes in solar output, the shifting continental positions, the uplift and erosion of mountain ranges and the development of the biosphere. No doubt orbital variations also occurred and affected climate, as well as volcanic eruptions and internal ocean changes, but we cannot find much evidence for such changes far back in time. It is only for the quite recent history of the Earth, especially the Quaternary period, that detailed, well-dated and continuous records of the past can be recovered, from many parts of the world, to help in deciphering how and why climates changed.

## Enquiry

1   Describe how the position of Antarctica has changed since the Jurassic period, 195 million years ago.

2   How would the climate of Antarctica have changed over this time? Look at the following website:

http://www.scotese.com

# Human influences on climate

## The rising tide of pollution

As society has gradually developed from the first hunter–gatherers to the enormous sprawling conurbations of today (a process that took around 4000 years), the scale of the environmental impact of human activities has grown from local to regional, and then from regional to global. This is well shown in Western Europe. Early villages had an influence on the immediate surroundings through the clearing of vegetation around each settlement to create farmland, the pollution of waterways and the local accumulation of waste products. But settlements were few and far between, which made their overall impact fairly limited.

As urban centres developed, pollution became more pervasive on a regional scale, especially during the 19th century, when water and air pollution became very serious problems. Choking smog was a common occurrence in cold winter months, as air stagnated over cities. With further urbanisation, a rising demand for energy and the tremendous growth of automobile use after about 1950, large-scale air pollution became widespread. This led to acid rain falling over wide areas, and contamination of lakes, rivers and estuaries – even in relatively remote areas. Furthermore, in order to provide fuel and land for agricultural use, deforestation has stripped huge areas of its natural vegetation cover.

Since the 1960s, some of these problems have been reduced, but not eliminated, particularly in Western Europe and North America. Legislation has required that reductions be made in air and water pollution, and that certain ecosystems be protected and conserved. Reforestation schemes have started and newly harvested forests replaced, sometimes on a 'two-trees-for-one' basis, albeit with a loss of biodiversity. In many less developed countries, however, the situation today is very much the same as it was in the more industrialised countries 100 years ago, especially in densely populated and rapidly mushrooming urban areas.

While it might appear that pollution is an issue that must be solved by individual countries, the fact of the matter is that pollution has assumed such dimensions as to make it a problem of global significance. This is especially true of air pollution, which has reached such levels that the global climate is being affected. The concentration of carbon dioxide ($CO_2$) in the atmosphere has increased by over 30 per cent in the past 150 years. This rising concentration is not confined to the air space over those countries that have produced it. In effect, we are returning to the

1 Why was so much coal burnt during the Industrial Revolution?

2 Why has coal consumption fallen since the middle of the 20th century?

3 Find out more about the Clean Air Act of 1956. Why was it introduced and how effective has it proved to be?

atmosphere the carbon dioxide that was removed and stored away as oil, coal and gas millions of years ago.

Methane ($CH_4$), another important greenhouse gas, has also greatly increased over the same period, due to the increase in rice cultivation, animal husbandry and other changes in the landscape that are related to agriculture. Methane is produced by decomposition under anaerobic conditions (in the absence of oxygen), such as is found in waterlogged rice paddies and in the intestines of animals. In addition, many other greenhouse gases have increased as a result of industrialisation. Gases that were once thought to be inert (chlorofluorocarbons) have had a devastating effect on ozone concentrations at very high levels in the atmosphere, leading to 'holes' appearing in the ozone layer in polar regions.

Unfortunately, the global impact of society on air pollution, and therefore on climate, is unlikely to go away. Indeed, it seems set to intensify, if only because population growth continues to accelerate at an extraordinary rate, pushing the global total to over 6 billion people by the start of the 21st century. Current projections indicate that the world population will double within the next 80–100 years. More people will mean more pollution, more environmental degradation and therefore more global climatic change.

**SECTION B**

# The record of atmospheric carbon dioxide

Detailed measurements of the carbon dioxide levels in the atmosphere began in 1957, in remote areas far from industrial society. It quickly became apparent that there is an annual cycle in $CO_2$ levels that reflects the 'breathing' of the global biosphere, with levels dropping in summer months as plants in the Northern Hemisphere begin to photosynthesise. However, in addition to this relatively minor 'wiggle' in the records on an annual basis, measurements soon revealed a more disturbing trend. Carbon dioxide levels were systematically rising from one year to the next, and the rate of increase was accelerating.

Today, we can look back on the overall series of measurements and see a clear picture of how $CO_2$ levels have changed over the past 100–200 years (**5.1**). Furthermore, measurements of $CO_2$ in gas bubbles extracted from Antarctic ice cores (which provide tiny samples of the atmosphere back in time) show that the increase in $CO_2$ began at the start of the Industrial Revolution, when coal was first used on a large scale. Today, $CO_2$ levels are more than 30 per cent higher than they were in the late 1700s, and the rate of increase is accelerating as the global consumption of fossil fuels continues to grow.

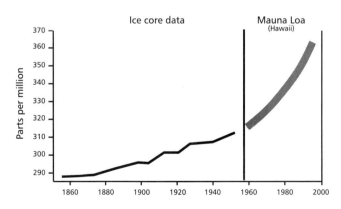

**Figure 5.1** The record of atmospheric $CO_2$ since the mid-19th century. Since 1957, the measurements are from instruments on the summit of Mauna Loa in Hawaii. Before that, the values are from air bubbles trapped in ice cores from Antarctica

It is extremely difficult to estimate how fast this concentration will increase in the future. It depends on many factors, such as:

- population growth
- changing standards of living
- the production of fuel-efficient motor vehicles
- the growth of public transportation systems
- the introduction of more energy-efficient building construction
- the development of other fuel systems, not based on carbon.

In addition, not all of the $CO_2$ produced by human activities stays in the atmosphere. Much of it is absorbed by the oceans, especially in the cooler waters of middle and high latitudes, where the gas becomes more soluble.

Anything that takes $CO_2$ out of the atmosphere and locks it away, even for a short time, is known as a **sink**. Current estimates show that around 40 per cent of all $CO_2$ produced from the combustion of fossil fuels is absorbed at the ocean surface. If that rate decreased, for example, by the oceans becoming warmer, this might increase the amount of $CO_2$ remaining in the atmosphere. Furthermore, since $CO_2$ is removed from the atmosphere by plants during photosynthesis, the expansion of forests and other ecosystems that can reduce atmospheric levels of the gas will also be important. In other words, the problem is not just a question of how much $CO_2$ will be produced from all sources, but also how much will be absorbed or removed via all of the sinks (**5.2**) (see also **Chapter 7 Section C**).

Given all of these uncertainties, it is not surprising that the projected changes in $CO_2$ for the future have wide margins of error. Nevertheless, all estimates show that by late in the 21st century, $CO_2$ levels are likely to reach twice the pre-industrial values. In 1800, $CO_2$ values were 270 ppmv

**Figure 5.2** Different estimates of how carbon dioxide levels in the atmosphere may change in the future, according to the Intergovernmental Panel on Climate Change

The large uncertainties exist because the numbers depend greatly on the assumptions made about population growth, energy use in the future, standards of living, the amount of natural forest that will be cut down, and what kinds of agriculture will be practiced in the future. All of these things are very uncertain, so the different estimates are, not surprisingly, quite varied. This makes it equally difficult to be certain about how climate may change in the future (see **5.7**).

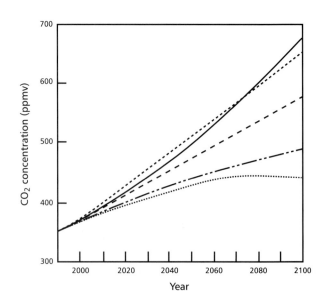

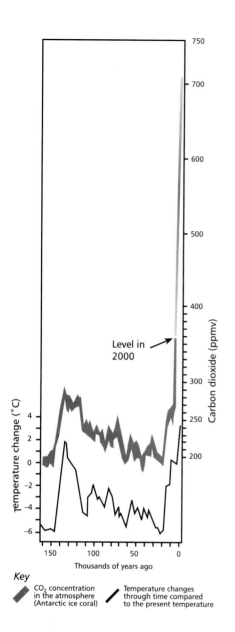

**Figure 5.3** The changes in atmospheric $CO_2$ over the past 150 000 years compared to changes expected to occur by 2100 or sooner

(parts per million by volume) (**5.2**). According to some estimates, the doubling could happen by as soon as 2050. Other estimates suggest that values could approach 700 ppmv by 2100. To put this in perspective, consider these changes in the context of the $CO_2$ record of the past 420 000 years, as seen in the ice-core records from Antarctica (**5.3**).

Clearly, $CO_2$ concentrations will soon rise to levels not seen on Earth over the past 420 000 years, and the rate of increase will be greater than anything experienced over the last glacial–interglacial cycle. In fact, if current rates of $CO_2$ increase continue, the concentration in the atmosphere will be greater than at any time during the past 10–15 million years. When we consider that the entire history of human evolution, from ape-like creatures to *Homo sapiens*, has taken place only within the last few million years, the enormity of what we are doing to the global atmospheric environment becomes clear. Even if effective measures are introduced straightaway to deal with the threat to global climate, it will take time before the situation is stabilised. So what effects will the growth in $CO_2$ levels have?

## Review

4   Explain why the carbon dioxide concentration in the atmosphere is expected to continue to increase, even though there is legislation to contain it.

5   Identify the main features shown in **5.3**.

---

**SECTION C**

# The record of global temperature

Measurements of temperature around the world have been made on a regular basis for the past 150 years or so, enabling a picture of global temperature changes to be built up. Figure **5.4** shows the record of mean annual temperatures since 1850. All values are expressed in relation to the average for 1961–1990, so years that were colder than this 30-year period have negative values, and warmer years have positive values. It is obvious from this record that temperatures have risen over the past 150 years, reaching their highest levels in the 1990s. In fact, new record highs were reached several times in the 1990s.

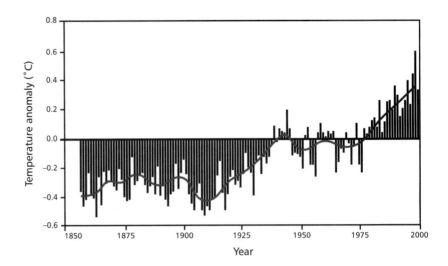

**Figure 5.4** The average annual temperatures for the Earth, based on instrumental measurements on land and on ships, since about 1850

The values are shown in relation to the average from 1961 to 1990, so years with lower temperatures are negative. The running mean is shown as a thick wavy line.

Many studies have argued that this warming is due to the build-up of greenhouse gases in the atmosphere. However, other research has questioned this conclusion. Critics point out that the warming has not been continuous, and that the temperatures were relatively stable from the 1940s to the mid-1970s, while $CO_2$ levels continued to rise (**5.4**). Recent studies appear to resolve this problem by showing that the reduction in warming in the period 1940–1970 was due to the presence of other atmospheric pollutants. Small particles (especially sulphates) have also been produced on a massive scale as a by-product of industrial processes, particularly since the end of the Second World War. These caused a reduction in the amount of solar radiation reaching the Earth's surface, and the resulting cooling counteracted the warming due to $CO_2$ and other greenhouse gases.

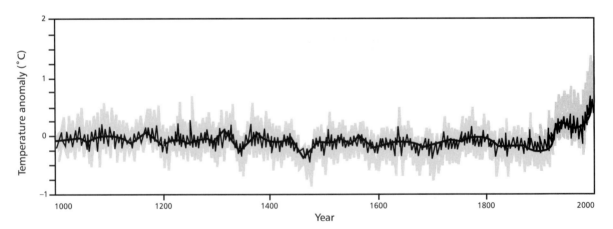

**Figure 5.5** An estimate of average annual temperatures for the Northern Hemisphere, since AD 1000

The annual values are shown in relation to the average from 1902 to 1980, so years that were colder than that period are negative values. A running mean of the variations is shown as a thick wavy line and light shading indicates the level of uncertainty in the temperature estimates. These estimates are based on a wide variety of paleoclimatic data, from tree rings, corals, historical records and ice cores, so there is an uncertainty associated with each yearly value. This is shown as a grey shaded area surrounding the overall curves.

## Review

6 Examine the effects that the following might have on global temperatures:

- volcanic eruptions

- increasing industrialisation

- clearance of the tropical rainforest.

7 Explain how some atmospheric pollutants can reduce global temperatures.

Since the mid-1970s, the continuous build-up of $CO_2$ has led to the warming effect becoming dominant, and this explains why temperatures have risen compared to the situation in the previous few decades (**5.4**). The warming in the 20th century is even more obvious when a longer-term record is examined. Figure **5.5** shows an estimate of Northern Hemisphere mean annual temperatures over the past 1000 years, based on studies of climate-related proxy records, such as tree rings, ice cores, corals and so on (see **Chapter 3**). The warming in the 20th century was clearly quite unusual compared to the previous 900 years, bringing to an end a long-term cooling trend. In fact, this record shows a quite rapid change, from one of the coldest periods of the past 1000 years, in the early 19th century, to the warmest period, in the 1990s.

Further studies of the data in **5.5** show that, for the period up to the late 1800s, most of the variations can be explained by small changes in the output of the Sun, and by explosive volcanic eruptions that led to a haze of fine particles being spread across the Earth, reducing incoming radiation. However, in the 20th century, these factors became overwhelmed by the effect of the excess greenhouse gases resulting from the combustion of fossil fuels and deforestation around the world. At least 50 per cent of the 20th-century warming appears to have been the result of these increases in greenhouse gases, with the balance of the warming due to an increase in solar radiation and a relatively small number of volcanic eruptions over the past 100 years (**5.6**).

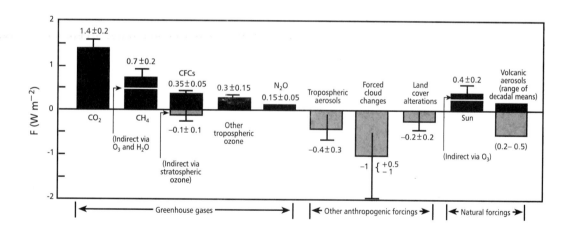

**Figure 5.6** Estimates of the different factors affecting climate ('climate forcings') between 1850 and 2000

Values are given in watts per square meter, which is a measure of the overall change in the energy balance of the atmosphere. Positive values indicate that the effect has been to warm the Earth's climate, and negative factors indicate cooling. The vertical lines on each column represent the uncertainty of the estimates. The largest uncertainties are about the role of clouds and how they are affected by aerosols produced by human activity.

# Climate in the near future

Unless energy use changes radically and quickly, it is almost certain that the levels of greenhouse gases will rise further in the 21st century as world population continues to grow, and overall standards of living increase (requiring more and more energy consumption).

A critical question is: How will such changes affect global climate? To answer this, climatologists employ sophisticated computer models of atmospheric and oceanic circulation. These models use mathematical equations to simulate processes that are involved in energy exchange and other processes that control world climate. Typically, a model will produce a simulation of many years of climate, and the conditions in the final few decades of the model simulation will be averaged to compare with modern climate data. Although the simulations are not perfect, they do manage to reproduce the observed pattern of climate around the world quite well. They reproduce temperature patterns particularly well, but are weakest in showing an accurate picture of snowfall and rainfall patterns, mainly because they do not simulate cloud variations very accurately. Nevertheless, the models are improving all the time, and they are now considered to be adequate for use in estimating how climates may change in the future (**5.7**).

The results of most of these simulations indicate that global temperatures are likely to increase dramatically this century, to levels far higher than

**Figure 5.7** The changes in temperature over the past 1000 years (as shown in **5.5**) compared to the changes expected over the next 100 years, because of the enhanced greenhouse effect (see the caption to **5.5**)

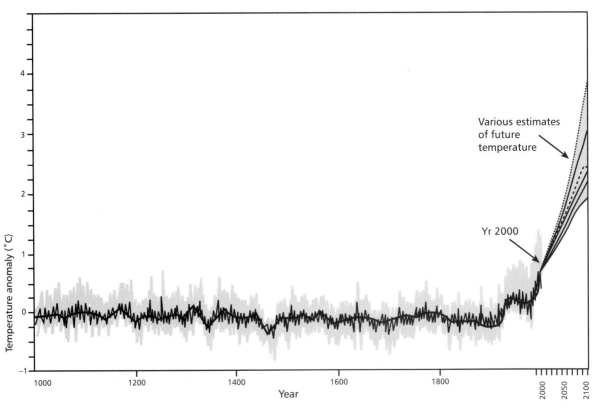

**8 a** Make a list of the ways in which global climate is expected to change during the 21st century.

**b** For each of the changes that you have listed, suggest some of the effects that there will be on the environment.

anything recorded in recent times. It is worth noting that the warming will only be partly due to the radiative effect of the $CO_2$. Much of the warming will be due to secondary factors, such as the increase in water vapour (another greenhouse gas) and changes in sea-ice, snow cover and clouds. All of these will tend to reinforce the direct radiative influence of the higher levels of $CO_2$ – a case of positive feedbacks. It is clear that even if one takes the lower estimates of future temperature change, the climate is likely to be altered to an extent that is not apparent in data spanning at least the past 1000 years.

Most models also indicate that global warming will have knock-on climatic effects overall. For example, while global precipitation will increase, the distribution of rainfall and snowfall may change dramatically. As temperatures rise, the hydrological cycle will be enhanced, leading to more moisture being carried to high latitudes, increasing precipitation, run-off, river discharge and the delivery of fresh water to the global ocean. Clearly, such changes, together with the rise in temperatures, pose real uncertainties about the viability of both natural ecosystems – such as are now preserved in many of the world's national parks – and the managed ecosystems of farmland and forests.

**SECTION E**

## Sea-level changes

One critical concern related to global warming is the extent to which sea level may change (**5.8**). Sea-level changes result from two factors:

- expansion of the water in the oceans as it gets warmer
- the melting of polar and mountain ice-caps.

**Figure 5.8** Sea-level change, 1750–2100

Current models suggest that sea level will rise as a result of global warming (compare with **5.7**). The uncertainties referred to in the text are reflected in the 'reference range' shown here.

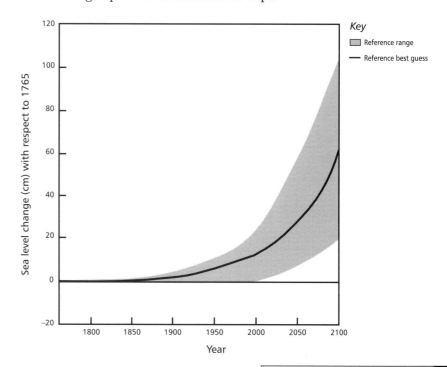

Although it may seem an unlikely cause of sea-level rise, the warming of the oceans has already resulted in an increase of 5 cm in global sea level during the 20th century. In addition, the melting of glaciers and ice-caps has contributed another 10 cm over the same period. Future sea-level changes are subject to the same uncertainties as noted earlier for climate simulations. Indeed, the estimates of whether glaciers will melt or grow, due to higher levels of snowfall, are largely based on the models of future climate conditions.

Current estimates indicate that the sea level will rise a further 30–50 cm over the next century (**5.8**). The biggest uncertainty in climatic prediction is whether a rise in sea level might cause ice shelves in western Antarctica to surge forward into the ocean, releasing a vast quantity of ice into the ocean. All of the ice in that part of Antarctica is equivalent to about 6 m of sea-level change. This is about the same amount as might be contributed by the ice over Greenland if it were to melt. Therefore, any change in the status of those ice sheets would have devastating consequences for coastal cities around the world. Currently, the scientific consensus is that sea-level changes in the near future will not involve surges of the polar ice sheets, but the issue remains a controversial one.

## Review

**9** Explain the significance of the shaded area in **5.8**.

**10** Why has warming of the oceans led directly to a rise in sea level? (Refer to **Chapter 6** and the section on the 'steric' rise of sea level.)

SECTION F

# Chlorofluorocarbons and the ozone hole

Until quite recently, many spray cans and most air-conditioning units in cars, as well as refrigerators, contained a type of chlorofluorocarbon chemical (CFC). At one time, it was considered to be inert; that is, it was thought not to react with other materials. However, in the 1970s this was discovered to be false. In fact, these chemicals have two important and detrimental characteristics:

- They are very efficient greenhouse gases. Molecule for molecule, they absorb more long-wave radiation than many other greenhouses gases.
- They are highly reactive with ozone ($O_3$). Ozone is a critical gas, because it absorbs ultraviolet radiation in the stratosphere (the upper atmosphere).

High levels of ultraviolet radiation are known to cause skin cancer and cell mutations. Therefore, a reduction in stratospheric ozone would be very harmful to life on Earth. Furthermore, when ozone absorbs incoming ultraviolet radiation, it heats up the layers where it is found and so affects the vertical temperature gradients in the atmosphere.

Over the past few decades, CFCs have spread through the atmosphere and reacted strongly with ozone. Fortunately, the serious nature of the problem was recognised, and an international agreement – the Montreal Protocol – was signed in 1987. This phased out the use of ozone-depleting chemicals over a short period. The bad news is that high levels of chlorofluorocarbons remain in the atmosphere, and it will be decades before they disappear. In the meantime, ozone depletion continues to be a problem, with serious reductions taking place annually, especially over Antarctica and the Arctic. These reductions are commonly referred to as **ozone holes**, and satellite observations reveal that an area of greatly reduced ozone levels develops each year during the spring in both the Antarctic and the Arctic.

Ozone loss is at a maximum in the spring months because, during the long polar night, atmospheric circulation over the Poles is very restricted and temperatures can commonly fall to below –80°C in the upper atmosphere. At these very low temperatures, special clouds form: these contain nitric acid droplets, which react with the chlorofluorocarbon compounds in the air. When the Sun returns to the polar regions in the spring, the sunlight then causes these molecules to split. The resulting chemicals are highly reactive with ozone, causing its rapid removal from the atmosphere. You can track changes in the ozone hole and learn more about the problem at the following website:

http://www.atm.ch.cam.ac.uk/tour/index.html

produced by the Centre for Atmospheric Science (Cambridge University).

In recent years, each Antarctic spring has revealed another large loss of ozone, and the area of ozone depletion has sometimes extended as far as Australia, causing much concern over higher levels of ultraviolet radiation and its potential for increasing the occurrence of skin cancer. In the Northern Hemisphere, ozone loss over the Arctic has also increased in recent years, and there are similar concerns over the possibility that rates of skin cancer may increase as a result. This problem is slowly being brought under control by the Montreal Protocol, so the ozone-depleting chemicals that have accumulated in the atmosphere over past decades will eventually be removed and the ozone balance in the atmosphere will be restored. In the meantime, these chemicals contribute to global warming.

Summing up, then, it seems clear that increased population growth and the relentless demand for more carbon-based fuel will inevitably lead to higher levels of greenhouse gases in the atmosphere during the 21st century. Within the lifetime of everyone who is reading this, atmospheric concentrations of $CO_2$ will reach record levels. Not only will global temperatures rise, but there will also be significant shifts in the global amount and distribution of precipitation. World leaders generally focus on short-term, geographically limited political issues: very few of them have started to come to grips with this long-term global problem. The Kyoto Protocol (see **Chapter 8**), although far from perfect, was an important step towards addressing the problem at an international level, but until even more radical changes are made to our current production of greenhouse gases, we can continue to expect significant changes in climate.

In January 2001, the IPCC held a major meeting in Shanghai to issue its strongest advice yet that global warming is fact, not supposition. The United Nations responded by agreeing that the effects of global warming, as detailed in this book, 'are potentially devastating' and that the international community needed to come together to attack the causes in a way that, up to that point, it had not. The meeting was attended by representatives of 99 countries, including the main oil producers. There was unanimous agreement to the findings. The joint Chairman said, 'Industry will see the logic of acting and although it will need incentives from government it will find itself being prompted by demands from customers. Drastic changes in lifestyle are not what we're talking about. There'll still be cars – but they will be much more efficient! I'm really optimistic that the report will lead to action.'

## Review

**11** Check that you understand the significance of the growing ozone hole in the context of climatic change.

**12** What evidence would you use to support the idea that the human contribution to global warming has increased in the past three decades?

**13** Why was the 1987 Montreal Protocol such an important agreement for the Earth and its people?

## Enquiry

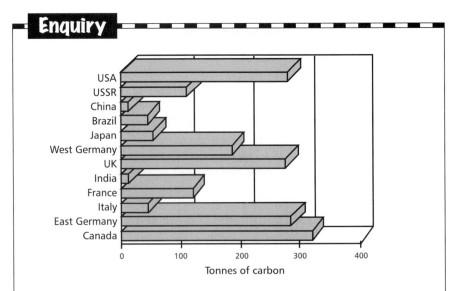

**Figure 5.9** Per capita $CO_2$ production in selected countries, 1860–1986

Study the data in 5.9. Explain how the growth of world population and changing patterns of industrial production will affect the distribution of greenhouse gas emissions.

# Environmental effects of climatic change

## Unusual and extreme weather events

The year 1999 was dominated by extreme weather events. In January, Toronto experienced its worst snowstorms since records began in this Canadian city. In February, there were also very heavy snowstorms in the Alps, the worst in 40 years. They led to avalanches in Switzerland and Italy, while a tourist village was obliterated in Austria. In March, Cyclone Vance caused major damage in Western Australia. April in New Zealand saw the end of the second of two severe droughts that followed one another closely. May brought the worst drought in living memory to Mexico, with a serious consequences for the grain harvest. Each month of the year brought new examples of extreme weather somewhere on the planet, many of them of greater extent or severity than ever before. The year ended with a crescendo of extreme weather events and an estimated world total of some 25 million environmental refugees, mainly as a result of weather-related problems.

As the factors that affect climate are changed, by either natural or human agencies, one of the first things to happen at a given location is that weather events become less reliable and more extreme. This may be because the distribution of climatic patterns changes, so that an area comes under the influence of a different climatic regime. For example, with global warming the Paris Basin may well begin to experience a climate more typical of areas south of the Pyrenees today.

## Case study: The increasing risk of extreme events

Every year, in some location or another, extreme weather events occur. But the recent spate of unusual weather conditions around the world has led insurance companies to express concern that the climate is now less predictable than it was. After all, when disasters take place, it is the insurance companies that have to pay out large sums of money to those people who are insured with them. For further information, see the following website:

http://epa.gov/global warming/

Caught in the recent past by an increasing number of claims from householders following storm damage or flooding, the insurance industry has put a lot of effort into attempting to quantify their new climatic risks. Accurate and detailed weather readings have been taken at some sites for over 150 years. Simply graphing such data can often be revealing. For example, **6.1a** shows the distribution of mean summer temperatures in southern England between 1961 and 1990. The graph tells us that the mean summer temperature was 15.3°C. Years with a temperature mean of 17.3°C or above occurred very infrequently, and this is illustrated by them being in the right-hand 'tail' of the normal curve. The probability of a summer mean temperature of 17.3°C or more was only 1.3 per cent per annum.

**Figure 6.1** The effect of a change in mean temperature: temperature curves with a mean of (**a**) 15.3°C and (**b**) 16.9°C. Just a small increase in mean temperature can lead to a much greater likelihood of the occurrence of extreme temperatures

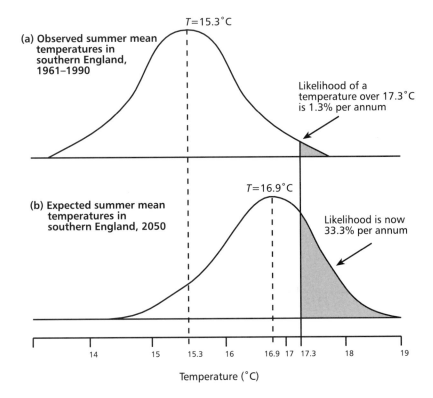

(a) Observed summer mean temperatures in southern England, 1961–1990

*T*=15.3˚C

Likelihood of a temperature over 17.3˚C is 1.3% per annum

(b) Expected summer mean temperatures in southern England, 2050

*T*=16.9˚C

Likelihood is now 33.3% per annum

Temperature (˚C)

Let us suppose that the average temperature increases so that the summer mean becomes 16.9°C, a modest rise of 1.6°C, less than half the change predicted for the next 50 years or so (**6.1b**). There is still a normal distribution of mean temperatures, but centred now around a mean of 16.9°C. The likelihood of a temperature mean of 17.3°C or more being recorded has become 33.3 per cent per annum. This means that with a rise of just 1.6°C in mean temperature, the likelihood of an extreme of 17.3°C has increased by a factor of about 25 (to be exact, 33.3 divided by 1.3). Just a small shift in mean temperature has increased the likelihood of hitherto extreme events quite considerably.

The insurance industry is constantly revising its calculations in the face of changing climatic conditions, in order that it does not charge premiums that are either too high, so that nobody pays them, or too low, thereby putting its ability to pay in times of crisis at risk. Without necessarily blaming human influence for the recent changes in climate, there is no doubt – in the insurance industry's view – that changes are occurring, and that they will have dramatic economic consequences.

Figure **6.2** shows some of the risks associated with changes in other meteorological parameters from the point of view of an insurance company. The insurance industry would be expected to pick up the bill for a lot of the climatic events discussed, so it would need to be aware of any significant increase in risk.

**Figure 6.2** Some increased risks associated with climatic change

Figure **6.3** lists a number of observed or expected changes that may be linked with global warming. The changes are ranked in order of scientific certainty.

| Meteorological parameters | Relevant extreme values | Effects | Classes of insurance affected |
|---|---|---|---|
| Temperature | Absolute daily maximum | Heat wave | Health, life, commercial |
| | Monthly/seasonal maximum | Heat wave, drought, pests, disease | Health, life, agriculture |
| | Daily/monthly maximum | Frost, ice | Health, agriculture, buildings, damage to cars |
| Rain | Hourly/daily maximum | Storm surge | Buildings, commercial, damage to cars, engineering, cancellation of events |
| | Weekly/monthly maximum | Flood | Buildings, commercial, agriculture |
| | Monthly/seasonal maximum | Drought, subsidence | Agriculture, buildings |
| Wind | Absolute/hourly maximum Speed/frequency | Windstorm (severe storm, tornado, tropical cyclone, windstorm, storm surge) | Buildings, commercial, damage to vehicles, aviation, marine, engineering, cancellation of events |
| Hail, lightning | Frequency | Impact | Buildings, commercial, damage to vehicles, aviation, marine, engineering, cancellation of events |

| Degree of scientific certainty | Effect of global warming |
| --- | --- |
| Very high | An increase in global mean temperatures in the lower atmosphere and in the upper ocean layers. |
| | A decrease in global mean temperature in the stratosphere. |
| | Temporarily severe ozone destruction in the polar stratosphere (ozone hole). |
| | A decrease in the global ozone concentration in the stratosphere. |
| | The melting and retreat of inland glaciers and polar ice. Polar bears starve as the ice melts. They can no longer stalk their main prey – seals – on the sea-ice. |
| | Extended periods of drought and an increase in forest fires. |
| High | Accelerated sea-level rise. The risk of flooding in heavily populated coastal lowlands such as Bangladesh and the Nile delta. The Everglades may be partly inundated. |
| | An increase in atmospheric turbidity (aerosols) in some regions, with cooling effects on the atmosphere. |
| | An increased frequency of mild winters with poor snow cover in Central Europe. A threat to an important winter sport industry. |
| | Increased winter rainfall in Central Europe (decrease in Southern Europe). Irrigated agriculture under stress. |
| | Increasing winter storm activity over the North Atlantic. Severe damage likely in coastal regions. |
| Low | Increasing winter storm activity in Western and Central Europe. |
| | Increasing tropical windstorm activity (frequency, intensity, source area and duration of storm season). |
| | Increasing activity of thunderstorms, torrential rainfall and hailstorms in moderate climates. |
| | Changes in fauna and flora. The Arctic tundra begins to thaw: birds such as geese, sandpipers, dunlins and stints are in severe danger as their breeding grounds change in character and their winter feeding grounds (coastal marshes) are inundated. |
| | An expansion of drought and desert zones in subtropical climates. Changes are required to traditional farming systems. |
| | The spread of tropical diseases, such as malaria, yellow fever, dengue fever and encephalitis. |

**Figure 6.3** The possible effects of global warming

**SECTION B**

# Melting ice and sea-level change

One of the most predictable results of global warming is, or will be, the melting of polar ice.

## Case study: The thinning of ice at the North Pole

In March 1959, an American submarine was the first to surface through the ice at the North Pole. To do so, it had to break through thick sea-ice. Since then, a succession of submarines has done likewise and the records – both from this source and from remote satellite sensing – suggest that a steady thinning has occurred. When a Russian ice-breaker took a party of tourists to the North Pole in August 2000, the nearest patch of ice capable of bearing a person's weight was some 9 km from the Pole. Large areas of ocean were either clear or covered only by very thin ice.

The Scott Polar Research Institute in Cambridge estimates the ice to have thinned by some 40 per cent between 1970 and 2000. It also estimates that, within 50 years, the Arctic Ocean will be completely ice free during the northern summer. This is potentially calamitous for animals such as the polar bear, which needs a long, harsh winter. Whereas the ecological effects will be devastating, the same melting will mean that northern trade routes will open up, making it possible to ship cargoes, such as bulk grain and oil, between North America, Europe and Asia by much shorter routes than are presently possible.

## Case study: Global warming and disruption of the Antarctic marine food web

In Antarctica, some animals – such as Adelie and Emperor penguins and crabeater and Ross seals – live all of their lives on the ice or in the seas directly surrounding it. The nutrient-rich seas that directly surround the ice are ideal for the growth of phytoplankton (single-celled plants).

Zooplankton (tiny animals such as krill, and the young of larger species) graze this rich food source. These, in turn, support a large population of fish, which are then eaten by penguins and seals. As the frozen area shrinks, so the sea-ice boundary (the zone of highest marine productivity) will change in location, disrupting the present distribution of marine flora and fauna. The long-term effect of such a change is unclear, but if – as appears very likely – these changes happen rapidly (over a few decades), they would probably be very disruptive to the marine ecosystems of Antarctica.

Figure **6.4** shows the food web of the southern oceans and demonstrates the delicate nature of the system.

**Figure 6.4** A food web in the southern oceans. A very rich ecosystem depends on the rich mineralised waters found around the ice margins. The phytoplankton (plant plankton) is grazed by the krill, which are the basic food for many species

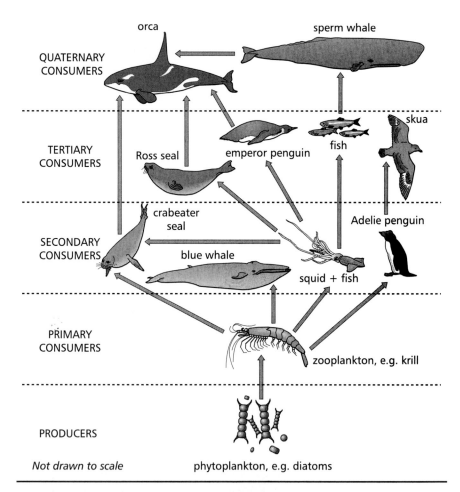

orca

sperm whale

QUATERNARY CONSUMERS

skua

TERTIARY CONSUMERS

Ross seal

emperor penguin

fish

crabeater seal

Adelie penguin

SECONDARY CONSUMERS

blue whale

squid + fish

PRIMARY CONSUMERS

zooplankton, e.g. krill

PRODUCERS

*Not drawn to scale*   phytoplankton, e.g. diatoms

As we have seen, the sea level at the end of the last ice age was 120 m lower than today, because of the amount of water locked up on the continents in the form of ice sheets. Since then, the sea level has risen steadily, but it has been fairly stable for the past few thousand years. With a more stable sea level, life can gradually adjust to the new circumstances, as illustrated by the adjustment of living coral and the formation of coral reefs and atolls (**6.5**). It is when processes of change are very rapid that they can overwhelm the flora and fauna. A predicted rise in sea level of some 30–50 cm over the next century could be too rapid to be accommodated by the world's coral reefs.

**Figure 6.5** The growth of a coral atoll, related to changing sea levels. The relatively slow change in sea level since the ice age has led to the growth of new islands. In the future, coral may not be able to keep pace with a more rapidly changing sea level

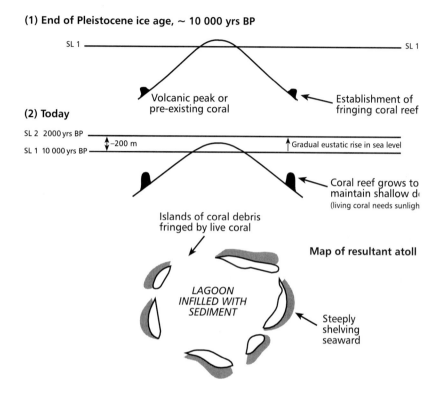

Another factor that affects sea-level change is related to the temperature of the oceans themselves. As temperatures continue to rise, so the ocean water itself expands, a component known as **steric adjustment**. This is of minor significance on a long time-scale, but it becomes important when we try to understand recent sea-level changes, and to estimate how the sea level may change in a future of rapidly rising temperatures. The expanding water column adds to the overall sea-level rise that results from melting glaciers and ice sheets.

Coral not only needs shallow, clear water in which to grow, but it also reacts sensitively to water temperature. Once that temperature goes above 32°C, the symbiotic relationship between coral and algae breaks down. The coral becomes bleached and dies. Records from Suva, the capital of Fiji, indicate that there was a net rise in temperature of some 0.5°C between 1884 and 1986. This fits in with the warming records quoted elsewhere in this book, and helps to explain why the sea level in the Pacific has been rising since at least 1884 – and probably for 100 years before that. Actual records are hard to come by, but the older inhabitants of the Pacific islands all tell the same story:

- shorelines have advanced

- land has been lost
- coastal vegetation, such as mangroves and coconut palms, has been destroyed.

Measurements from tidal gauges around the Pacific suggest that the sea level has risen by about 1.5 mm per year over the past 100 years. This does not seem a lot to us, but consider the fact that many of the islands – in Kiribati, the Marshall Islands, Tokelau and Tuvalu, for example – rise no more than 4 m above sea level. If the climate warms as rapidly as predicted (see **5.5**), then the gradual, almost imperceptible rise of sea level that has happened up to now will accelerate. The twin effects of sea-level rise and warming may mean that coral would not be able to adapt to such rapid change, causing it to die. The reefs that had afforded shelter would no longer do so and the islands would be exposed to storms. Given all the indications that the rate of warming is increasing, how much longer can such islands survive in their present form? Since some of the islands are the sole home of certain species of wildlife, such as the Hawaiian monk seal and Ridley's turtle, the future for many of the world's coral islands and their associated wildlife looks bleak.

## Review

**3** One possible outcome of the melting of the sea-ice around Antarctica is that the amount of phytoplankton could be greatly reduced. Make a sketch copy of **6.4** and annotate it to show the effect of such a scenario.

**4 a** Make a sketch copy of **6.5** and add notes to show how the growth of coral islands has been facilitated by a gradual rise in sea level.

**b** Add a further sketch to show what may happen if there is a relatively sudden rise of sea level by 50 mm each year for the next 100 years.

# Forest fires and changes in wildlife distribution

Global warming will also lead to an increased risk of forest fires (**6.3**). Climate models suggest that droughts will increase in frequency in many areas, and that this will bring about a consequent increase in the likelihood of fires. Exceptionally dry conditions prevailed in various parts of the world during 2000, causing devastating fires in Cyprus and Greece, in the western USA, in Australia and in northeastern Siberia. There is further useful information at the following website:

http://www.noaa.gov/fireweather/

# Case study: Forest fires in the USA in 2000 - a sign of things to come?

As a prelude to what might be expected, consider the fires that wreaked havoc in the western states of the USA in the summer of 2000. There are fires every year in the remote coniferous forests of Wyoming, Idaho and California, often set off by lightning. However, in 2000 the scale of the fires was so enormous that the fire-fighters had to resort to evacuation rather than attempting to control them.

The difference between 2000 and previous years was explained by the weather that led up to the fires. There had been significant droughts, which had desiccated the vegetation, brushwood and litter. On 18 August 2000, a satellite image of Idaho and western Montana showed 17 very large forest fires burning out of control. Just 22 days later, after several days of cooler temperatures, higher humidities and even rain and snow in some areas, just one fire was left burning. None of the fires had been extinguished by fire-fighting teams. Without this change in the weather, the fires would have become even more widespread.

The weather conditions alone dictated the number and extent of the fires. Fire Departments in the USA use a **drought index** to monitor the susceptibility of vegetation to fires. The index ranges from 0 (no drought) to 800 (extreme drought). In computing this index, the following factors are taken into account:

- maximum daily temperature
- daily precipitation
- antecedent precipitation (the amount and intensity of precipitation in the preceding period)
- annual temperature.

The index is typically at its highest in autumn, when there is a lot of freshly fallen litter and a water deficit after the summer period. In August 2000, the index was between 670 and 800. As global warming takes effect, there is the prospect, in this region, of even high index values and of more frequent fire disasters like those of the summer of 2000.

Certainly, this case study, and other examples discussed earlier, paint a rather depressing picture of potential future environmental degradation due to global warming. However, there may also be some positive effects. For example, some vegetation has recently been able to colonise areas where it was previously unable to grow.

Trees are very sensitive to temperature conditions, so the height of their upper limit of colonisation (the tree line) is a good indicator of change. The analysis of tree stumps, left in the ground after the death of the tree, can

**Figure 6.6** The changing tree line in the northern Urals. Trees were able to grow on much higher slopes in the warmer period of 1100–1200, whereas the lower temperatures of the Little Ice Age led to a decline in height of the tree line

give a good idea of the changes that have occurred over time. Tree-trunk evidence tells us that the altitude of the tree line in many areas of the world has been rising. For example, **6.6** shows the height of the tree line in the northern Ural mountains, revealing that over the past 1200 years there have been times when trees grew at much higher altitudes than they do today. However, the tree line declined after about 1200 and reached its lowest elevation in about 1750, during the so-called Little Ice Age. Since about 1950, there has been a rapid expansion of the area under trees, and the elevation of the tree line continues to rise as global temperatures increase. Wildlife associated with the mountain forest growth will also benefit from this expansion.

As a result of changes in climate, some species of fauna are not only re-colonising former occupied areas but are also colonising entirely new ones. The blackcap is a small bird that was once a summer visitor to the British Isles. It is now increasingly staying in the country all year round, as mean winter temperatures increase. Little egrets have now colonised many inlets and wetlands in southern England, whereas before 1970 they were very rare vagrants. Accidental introductions may also flourish. A colony of rock wallabies lives happily in the Peak District, and exotic ring-necked parakeets breed in the parks around Twickenham, in the western suburbs of London. Global warming also gives farmers in the UK the chance to grow a wider range of crops, such as maize and vines.

While these may be seen as positive consequences of higher temperatures, unfortunately some pests and diseases may also take advantage of the changed conditions. Throughout the UK, lilies are now threatened by the bright red lily beetle, and pot plants have been decimated by the voracious root-eating grubs of the vine weevil. Neither pest was known in the UK before about 1980. In other areas, such as New York, disease has become a

## Review

5 Give some examples of the economic opportunities that might be created by global warming.

threat. In September 1999, an outbreak of mosquito-borne encephalitis occurred, after unusual weather conditions encouraged the carrier mosquitoes to breed there (although they possibly arrived via air transport rather than by natural migration). So climatic change leads to both beneficial effects and to the problematic spread of unwanted species.

## Flooding and desertification

Early in October 2000, South-East England suffered severe flooding. Uckfield in East Sussex was amongst the worst hit communities of all. Three days of incessant rainfall yielded totals that would be expected for the entire month of October. Added to the fact that it was falling on ground that was already sodden from considerable previous rainfall, flooding was inevitable. However, its effects were amplified by the fact that many new housing developments in the area had been built on the edges of the flood plain. Similar flooding occurred throughout the region and insurance companies were braced for claims totalling millions of pounds.

As well as being subjected to unprecedented rainfall, the South of England is gradually sinking. During the last ice age, the weight of ice tilted the north of the British Isles down, like a see-saw, with the south rising. Since the ice melted, isostatic readjustment has taken place. This means that, over the past 6000 years, the south of the British Isles has been gradually sinking to its pre-ice-age height. The result is an apparent rise in sea level and this add to the problems of drainage and the severity of flooding. (More information can be found in a companion volume, *The Fragile Environment: Pollution and Abuse*, by David Elcome.)

As climatic change takes place, rainfall patterns will shift. Some places will start to experience higher totals, and some lower. There will certainly be a different distribution of rainfall regimes. Flooding will become an increasing risk, especially around the mouths of rivers where floodwaters meet incoming high tides. As sea levels rise and storm surges increase, these places will face new threats, and the Uckfield experience will be repeated in places throughout the UK where there is not currently a problem with flooding. Given the changes expected in the locations of rainfall regimes, major flooding will also occur in places throughout the world where it has not been experienced before.

In stark contrast, other places will inevitably become much drier than at present – in fact, in some parts of the world, there is the prospect of **desertification**. This is the term used to describe the process whereby ecosystems become degraded, and begin to exhibit the classic features of arid or semi-arid zones. The symptoms include dwindling vegetation cover, as well as soil erosion by wind and flash flood. In addition, many of the world's existing arid regions have become even more severely desiccated. Although the process had been developing gradually, it first became headline news when a succession of very dry years in the 1970s led to major famines in the areas to the south of the Sahara in North Africa. This area, the Sahel, suffered enormous environmental degradation in a short time (**6.7**). Many thousands of square kilometres of land are now involved in this process, which is steadily causing the amount of semi-desert and desert cover around the globe to increase.

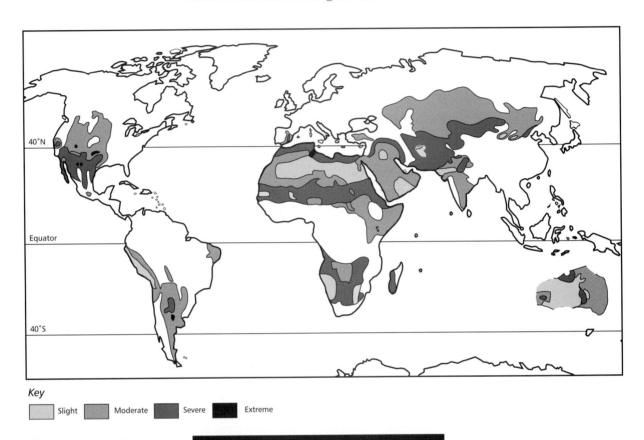

Key

Slight    Moderate    Severe    Extreme

**Figure 6.7** The global distribution of desertification. Large areas of the globe are already subject to long-term droughts and these may extend in the future as climate changes

## Case study: Desertification in Gujurat, India

A current example of environmental degradation associated with lower and less reliable rainfall comes from north-west India. Some 70 per cent of the tilled land in India is rain-fed, and Gujarat (along with the states of Orissa, Madhya Pradesh and Kerala) has received less than its usual share of an increasingly faltering monsoon season since 1990. The more severely affected areas of Gujarat include Rajastan, which borders the Thar Desert, one of the world's most arid areas. Around the fringes of the desert, the decrease in rainfall has been accompanied by desertification, the outward spread of desert conditions swallowing ever-larger areas of previously productive agricultural land. The reason for the spread of desert conditions is not necessarily purely climatic, although this usually plays a significant role. The process is exacerbated by other factors, as indicated in **6.8**.

**Figure 6.8** Factors affecting desertification. The effects of climatic change can be made worse by human activities

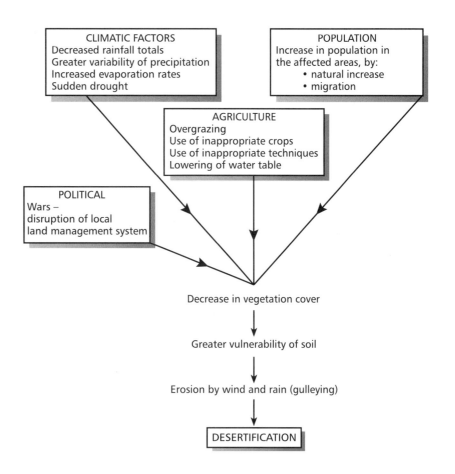

The farming activity in the area of Gujarat that is most severely affected by drought consists of mixed grain growing and cattle rearing. For many years, the farmers in the area have been able to rely on the monsoon rainfall, so they have had little need to irrigate the land. There are, however, many signs that the region was less dependent on this rainfall in the past. Ancient irrigation ponds and channels are found all over the area, and relate to a period when the monsoon rains were less reliable than in recent times. It appears that the climate has fluctuated in the past, but has now returned to a phase in which the rainfall is less predictable.

Some scientists suggest that desertification is really the result of human activity, superimposed on a natural cycle of changing rainfall variability. Increasing global temperatures lead to higher evapotranspiration rates. Rainfall may also become increasingly unreliable in many areas (**6.3**). Given that global population is also growing at a tremendous rate, land use will be under increasing stress, so it is very probable that desertification will be a significant threat in many areas. In Gujarat, measures are being taken to stem the advance of the drier conditions. Figure **6.8** shows that a lower water table is part of the problem. This is made worse by farming, which draws on the groundwater stores. Water storage facilities – ponds and tanks – are being resurrected and new ones installed to combat the shortage of water. Drought-resistant grasses and trees, such as acacia, are being planted to hold the soil together and prevent it from being blown away. More drought-tolerant grains are being grown, but problems still exist – such as a continued high level of grazing, which removes surface vegetation and leaves the soil open to erosion.

**Figure 6.9** One of the techniques used to halt the process of desertification is the preparation of windbreaks. Brushwood is planted, particularly along the crest lines of dunes, and this stays the rapid movement of surface sand.

Desertification is a widespread phenomenon, and the need to respond to it will generate an equally wide range of coping strategies, depending on the severity, the major local cause and the resources available to the country that is being affected. Meanwhile, climatic change will undoubtedly add to the extent and severity of the process throughout the world.

Data on global changes relevant to desertification can be found at the following website:

http://cdiac.esd.ornl.gov/trends/trends.htm

## Review

6 Describe the essential features of the distribution pattern shown in **6.7**.

7 Explain:

- how desertification shows us that the way the land is used can magnify the results of climatic change

- how land use may be a negative feedback that decreases desertification.

8 Make a list of the environmental effects that a rise in mean temperature might have on the British Isles. Classify those effects as being 'good', 'bad' or 'neutral'. How might people respond to those effects?

1 An atoll is just one physical feature that can indicate past changes in sea level:

   a   Refer to a physical geography textbook and identify two other physical features that indicate sea-level changes.

   b   Choose one of the features and find out what factors, other than sea-level change, contributed to its formation.

2 Study **6.10**, which shows the effects of climatic change on the vegetation of the British Isles over the past 18 000 years. Describe and explain how vegetation type and extent of coverage were linked to climate during this period.

| Approximate date | Climate of the British Isles | Effects on vegetation |
|---|---|---|
| Before 18 000 BC | The height of the Quaternary ice age. Ice sheets as far south as the Thames Valley. Valley glaciers in most hill areas north of this. | Very restricted patches of alpine vegetation in the south. No trees. |
| Around 18 000–12 000 BC | Gradual overall retreat of the ice front, but periodic colder and warmer spells mean halts, advances and retreats. | Gradual expansion of the area covered by alpine vegetation. No trees. |
| 12 000–10 000 BC | The retreat continues. Gradual warming, with relatively dry springs and early summers. | Alpine vegetation reaches lower altitudes. Few areas with no vegetation. |
| 10 000 BC | The climate continues to warm, but sudden cooling kills off trees, and glaciers re-establish themselves in the Lake District. | Birch trees grow in England. Alpine vegetation in mountain areas. Glaciers only in Scotland until the end of the period. Much of the British Isles is vegetated. |
| After 7800 BC | Gradual warming – the 'Boreal' phase. | Birches and pines, and then elms and oaks, spread from the south. More complex plant associations develop over much of the land. |
| After 6000 BC | The 'Atlantic' phase. Temperature on average 2°C warmer than today. High rainfall. | Trees and herbaceous plants spread widely from Europe. The sea level rises (as the ice sheets melt), causing the British Isles to become separated from continental Europe. Migrations of plant species are effectively halted, leaving the northern part of the continent with a wider range of trees than Britain. |

| Approximate date | Climate of the British Isles | Effects on vegetation |
| --- | --- | --- |
| 3500–1000 BC | The 'Sub-Boreal' phase. Temperatures slightly lower than in the previous period. Notably drier and less windy. | Birch and pine predominate in drier areas. Vegetation cleared from hilltops as settlements expand. |
| 1000–500 BC | Rapid re-establishment of a cooler, cloudier and wetter climate norm. | Birch increases in lowland areas, as do oaks and alders in wetter areas. Peats develop in upland areas. |
| AD 500–1000 | After a fluctuation (lower temperatures in Roman times), there is a warming and calming of conditions. | The great forests are established. |
| AD 1000–1250 | Storms less frequent than before or since. | The forests mature. |
| Around AD 1250 | Numerous storms and floods. | Forest damage is widespread. |
| AD 1550–1850 | The 'Little Ice Age' – much colder, with longer and more severe winters. | Alpine vegetation spreads in higher areas. The tree line descends. |
| After AD 1850 | Most of the period shows a gradual warming, but cooler periods still occur (for example, 1945–1970). | The conditions for tree growth spread (although agricultural use severely limits the extent of trees). |

**Figure 6.10** Recent climatic change and its effects on the vegetation of the British Isles

# Impacts on people and human responses

In **Chapter 6**, it was shown that climatic change will have dramatic impacts on the environment. It follows, then, that the effects on human activity will be no less wide-ranging. Given our present state of knowledge, it is difficult to predict exactly where the impacts and outcomes will be worst, but there is rather more certainty about the types of problem that will arise. This chapter looks at some of those problems and shows that, by monitoring events carefully, society may well be able to cope with the challenges as and when and where they occur.

The following website focuses on climate events and forecasts:

http://www.cpc.ncep.noaa.gov/index.html

**SECTION A**

## Responding to sea-level rise

Many countries around the world are seriously threatened by the sea-level rise that is predicted as a consequence of global warming. This rise is most likely to be in the region of 15 cm by 2050 and 34 cm by 2100 – although some estimates put the latter figure at nearer 1 m (the difference being explained by uncertainties about how the large ice sheets will respond to the warming). Along the east coast of the USA, the sea level has risen by an average of between 2.5 and 3.0 mm each year since 1990. It will be impossible to meet the costs of holding back the continually rising sea in all of the places where it threatens to inundate the land: however, there may be good reasons for taking action in selected regions. It has to be accepted that where a decision is made to implement coastal defensive works, there will probably be other major impacts.

### Case study: Managing sea-level rise in an American coastal city

Ocean City is a resort settlement on the Atlantic coast of Maryland (**7.1**). A cost–benefit analysis was commissioned by the city to find out whether it would be feasible and economically viable to protect it against flooding while maintaining the feature that attracted people there in the first place – the beach.

**Figure 7.1** A location map of Ocean City, Maryland

The principal reason for undertaking the analysis was financial. Much of the coastal land in Ocean City is valued at around US$2.5 million per hectare. It is certain that a rising sea level will mean stronger erosion forces and that these, in turn, will increase both the exposure of the coast to storm damage and the likelihood of coastal retreat. In the USA, damage of this sort can attract Federal disaster payments, so widespread coastal flooding may be expected to cost the nation a great deal of money.

In this analysis, the Ocean City experts examined two scenarios of possible sea-level rise. In the first case, an estimated sea-level rise of 30 cm per century (just like the current rate along this coast) was taken as the starting-point. The second scenario assumed an increase of 1.5 m over the same period, a mid- to high-level estimate, according to the US Environmental Protection Agency.

In the latter scenario, it was estimated that the sea-level rise between 1985 and 2025 would lead to a doubling of the rate of erosion along the coastline at Ocean City. This would equate to a coastline retreat of between 26 and 82 m if nothing were done to protect it. At present, sand is tipped at one end of the beach, to replenish it and protect it against erosion. It is then distributed naturally along the beach by longshore drift, while carefully spaced groynes hold back the sand to maintain a good beach width. At the present rate of sea-level rise, about 4 million cubic metres is dumped every year. In the second scenario, this would need to be increased to between 8 and 12 million cubic metres.

In the second scenario, in addition to upping the rate of sand dumping, erosion control would have to take precedence over recreational demands. As a result, access to the beach might become much more restricted. For example, at present the groynes leave long stretches of beach available for recreational activity. In the future, the sand would need to be dumped not just at one end of the beach, and in much larger quantities, but all the way along it. This is because the amount of sand that could be retained by the groynes would be insufficient to protect the coast against the inexorable rise of the sea. Increasing the supply of onshore sand might be done by pumping sand from the sea-bed some distance offshore, but a detailed study would be needed to find the least damaging source from which to obtain the sand.

With both of the sand replenishment rates discussed above, the protection scheme would be worthwhile, if only because the sums of money involved would be much less than the claims against Federal disaster funds if nothing were done. Similarly, if the costs are computed on a per visitor per year basis then, again, any intervention looks viable. Estimates for the higher rate of sand replenishment indicate that this would cost less than 50 cents per visitor each year.

Therefore, it could be argued that it would be worthwhile to protect this area of coast, but continued monitoring of the actual rate of sea-level rise, and evaluation of the acceptability of the defence strategy from a visual and safety point of view, would have to be carried out. If at any time the costs of the defence works looked likely to become much higher than the value of the benefits that might accrue, the whole scheme would have to be reassessed.

While the basic instinct may be to try to protect all threatened coastal areas, there are some good reasons why, on occasions, nothing should be done. For example, protection can lead to the loss of ecologically valuable coastal wetlands.

## Case study: Letting in the sea – for good reasons

In the UK, the Royal Society for the Protection of Birds (RSPB) put forward a plan in September 2000 to allow the controlled encroachment of the sea on coastal grazing land in Essex. The coastal marshes in Essex are wintering grounds for large numbers of waders, ducks and geese. The farmers concerned are bitterly opposed, and want the sea dykes to be strengthened to protect the Grade 1 agricultural land (the highest grade there is). If the dykes are built up, then the coastal marshes on the seaward side will be eroded, and will vanish altogether within 50 years. By contrast, controlled encroachment would enable the marshland ecosystem to move inland with the rising sea.

**Figure 7.2** The marshes of the Essex coast are very vulnerable to the rising sea level. It is important to manage the retreating coastline if the diversity of coastal ecosystems and the wildlife that it supports are to be maintained

The outcome of this particular example will probably rest on the financial power of the competing land users, as well as the attitude of the local planning authority. It needs to be stressed that, in this sort of situation, conservation can become competitive. The RSPB derives its income from public subscription (it has a membership of over 1 million) and revenues raised from visitors to its reserves. A nature reserve, such as this one on the Essex coast, can raise more money than many types of farming. Ironically, then, there may well be an increasing number of instances in which conservation calls the tune and the decision is made to let the sea in – albeit in a managed way.

As the sea level rises at a rate of between 3.0 and 5.0 mm per year, many of the low-lying Pacific Ocean coral island states, such as Kiribati and the Cook Islands, will become uninhabitable within 100 years or so. Much larger countries, such as the Netherlands and Bangladesh, will also be threatened. In the case of the Netherlands, there is a long and successful history of battling against the sea. Affordable technological answers may well be available there, but in the case of Bangladesh, it is difficult to see how the huge amounts of money required to defend the country could be raised. We can expect to witness frequent mass migrations of people as floods become more common and more severe. Since the vast majority of Bangladesh is so low-lying and highly susceptible to flooding, any migration would have to be cross-border, perhaps into India or Burma. Therefore, political problems may well be one of the knock-on effects of global warming and, as such, they represent the more alarming end of the impact spectrum.

## Review

1 Set out the main reasons for and against taking action to protect the coast from sea-level rise.

2 Explain why increased flooding in Bangladesh might lead to political problems.

3 What, if anything, do you think might be done to protect Bangladesh against the rise in sea level?

4 What criteria do you think should be used to decide which stretches of coastline should be given protection priority?

# Changes in the tundra and northern forests

The rising sea level will not be the only threat to mankind. Global warming will, by definition, affect every country on Earth and those effects will be felt in many different realms of human activity. Not all effects will be negative, but most will involve major challenges.

In a 1998 study, the US Environmental Protection Agency identified a number of ways in which regions would either benefit or suffer from the effects of climatic change. In their view, one region that will suffer is the northern sub-arctic region of North America. This region is currently covered by **taiga** (the northern forest) and **tundra**. The latter is underlain by permanently frozen ground known as **permafrost**, and consists of seasonal marshland and low-growing vegetation. Some of the permafrost is now melting, a process that has been linked with rising mean temperatures. At the present rate of melting, by the year 2050 the southern boundary of the permafrost will in all probability have moved north by 500 km.

**Figure 7.3** The taiga is one ecosystem that acts as a sink (a carbon dioxide store). Rising temperatures could change that

Vegetation in both the tundra and taiga is tough and acidic, meaning that litter from it only breaks down very slowly. This slowness is aided by the very short summers and frequently waterlogged conditions, factors that have led to the build-up of significant peat layers. This is one way in which carbon dioxide is stored away. These environments are currently net **sinks** for carbon dioxide. As the summers get warmer and the permafrost melts, surface water might drain away more easily, allowing the peat to dry out and decompose. This would cause $CO_2$ to be released to the atmosphere, and a net sink could then become a net source. In addition, the seasonal bogs that are so typical of tundra regions are the main breeding grounds for important migratory bird species, such as wildfowl and waders of many types. If the bogs were to drain over wide areas, this could have a major impact on these species. On the other hand, in areas where the terrain was suitable, melting permafrost could lead to even greater waterlogging and the further development of peat areas, locking up $CO_2$ in the vegetation. The exact impact of permafrost melting on the concentration of greenhouse gases in the atmosphere is therefore quite uncertain, and research is currently under way to determine more accurately which of these effects is likely to be the dominant one. In fact, this is true of many issues surrounding the impacts of greenhouse gas changes and global warming, and many scientists are focused on reducing these uncertainties.

Understanding the future is particularly important for the Inuit who live in these regions. There is concern that their lives will be seriously affected. Traditional society is based on harvesting the local natural resources, and for the Inuit these include caribou and salmon. Both species may suffer as the environment changes, putting extra stress on an already threatened lifestyle. In the case of caribou, for example, warmer winters may lead to rainfall events rather than snow. If rainfall occurs after snow covers the ground, the surface layer will become very hard, and it will be difficult for grazing animals such as caribou and musk oxen to break through to reach the tundra vegetation underneath. Case studies have shown that such conditions, which are rare today, can have a devastating impact on wildlife populations. If the frequency of such events were to increase, it might well lead to further impacts on traditional hunters in northern communities. Many Inuit have already settled in towns and cities: the pressure for still more to abandon their traditional way of life may well increase.

Further south in the USA, there are extensively forested areas. They are relatively lightly populated, but they provide important resources for the rest of the country, such as timber and wood pulp, and they also provide wilderness areas for tourism. As indicated in **Chapter 6**, these forests will become much more susceptible to fires as temperatures rise and humidities fall. Tree species adapted to the current climate regime may find it increasingly difficult to reproduce as the climate changes. Tree growth adjusts very slowly to new conditions, and the area covered by forests may therefore shrink. Consumer prices for timber would consequently rise. However, in the longer term (over several centuries), the area covered by forests may eventually increase significantly, bringing lower timber prices.

Economic uncertainty would thus accompany climatic change in the northern forested areas of the USA. The exploitation of these forest resources is organised from small towns set deep in the forests. The physical threat of fires and the economic problems of price instability could well lead to depopulation of those areas where the forest is most severely affected.

## Review

**5** Draw a flow diagram that traces through the impacts of permafrost thawing in the tundra.

**6** What actions might be taken to discourage depopulation of the northern forests?

# Coping with changing water resources

While global warming will lead to greater evaporation rates and overall higher rainfall on a global basis, the geographical patterns of rainfall will undoubtedly change too. Unfortunately, climate models are not yet good enough to predict which places will get more rainfall and which will get less. It is likely, however, that some important agricultural regions will find themselves with insufficient rainfall or irrigation water. On the other hand, some areas that are currently too dry for grain production may receive more rainfall, and eventually they could become important agricultural regions. This will require significant changes in the agricultural infrastructure, to support the planting and harvesting of new crops in areas where they are not grown at present. In some areas, the economic disruption associated with these changes will probably be associated with population movement, leading to political instability in some parts of the world where cross-border migration of people occurs.

**Figure 7.4** The Prairies of Canada. This area is the 'bread basket' of the Western world. What would happen if it became too dry to support the present level of wheat production?

## Review

7 Think through some of the human consequences of changes in the distribution of snow. What benefits would there be for mountainous areas which previously had little or no snow, and for agricultural areas on the plains below the mountains?

Reservoirs that serve urban areas in regions of increasing aridity may need to be re-engineered to collect more rainfall. Steps may also have to be taken to reduce evapotranspiration and enhance run-off to the reservoirs. In other areas, dams may be too small to retain the run-off from higher rainfall amounts, requiring further engineering solutions. These examples serve to illustrate the general point that global warming involves more than just changes in temperature, and some of the more difficult problems are likely to involve changes in rainfall (and snowfall) patterns. To support your work on water resources and drought, see these useful websites:

http://enso.unl.edu/ndmc/

http://www.drought.noaa.gov

# Responses in agriculture and other activities

The most important farming regions will feel the greatest impact from climatic change. Farmers are amongst the most adaptable of people, already being used to altering crop choice according to weather and changing market conditions. However, the predicted northward movement of crop belts will put them under even greater strain. The more mechanised a farming system is, the less it depends on the weather. For example, when harvesting has to be completed in wet conditions, the grain can still be dried mechanically to save it from rotting.

Figure **6.3** showed that, as global warming progresses, the projected spread of drought conditions in semi-tropical areas and the associated problems for traditional farming systems are less certain than current predictions of melting polar ice or increased forest fires. However, there are signs that traditional farming in some areas is already coming under threat. The environment of the coastal region of Gujarat in India (near the borders with Pakistan) has recently suffered from severe weather fluctuations – see the case study on page 72. Up until about 1990, the monsoon rains arrived with regularity and predictability. As well as affecting the environment, climatic change in Gujarat has impacted on people living in the area. The prosperity of this farming region was founded on groundnuts and soya beans, but in recent years the monsoon rains have appeared only in about one year in two, the cumulative deficit being more than half of normal expectations.

**Figure 7.5** Gujarat has many areas where farming has been carried on for a long time. The scenery is a patchwork of arable fields, divided by stone walls. Normally the crops are watered by the monsoon rains but in the last few years rainfall totals have been much lower, necessitating the artificial irrigation of crops.

In India as a whole in 1998, only 64 per cent of the country's cultivable land received sufficient rain. The rains have been late or less than anticipated since 1990, and so the farmers have not planted the traditional groundnuts, a profitable and high-yielding crop. Instead, they have opted for less nutritious grains such as sorghum, or even pulses such as lentils. The decline in crop quality is being accompanied by other unwanted side-effects. Fodder is generally of very poor quality, but it is grazed by the many cattle that form part of the subsistence farming system. The cattle remove the vegetation cover, leaving the soil exposed to wind and to heavy rains (when they do come). The soil is eroded by wind, which removes the finer particles, leaving only coarser, less fertile soil in the fields. Rainfall results in gullying and a further loss of soil.

Many villages in Gujarat have rain storage systems, tanks and ponds. These were mainly built 200–300 hundred years ago, when a previous dry climate gripped the region. They had gone out of use because the monsoon rain had become much more reliable since the middle of the 19th century and irrigation was no longer needed. They are now being revived in an attempt to keep the farms in production.

Much of the agriculture in the USA is highly mechanised. Although there is less concern about year-to-year variations in the weather than in farming in many other parts of the world, since mechanisation increases the ability to respond, variations in the climate are a different matter. They affect what can be grown in the long term and the optimum type of land management. Just as in Gujarat, farmers can cope with the occasional drought year, but they will have much more difficulty in dealing with completely different climate regimes. The rate of change predicted for the climate of the Great Plains, for example, is much faster than ever before. This calls into question the ability of farmers to adapt. In particular, unreliability of water resources will pose a serious threat to crop yields in those areas that are not used to large-scale irrigation.

On the positive side, an increase in the atmospheric concentration of $CO_2$ will increase crop yields. Cotton, soya and wheat are all expected to benefit from yields that may be up to 30% higher than now. However, this advantage will disappear as soon as drought conditions affect the Great Plains, as is predicted by climate models. In addition, farmers' traditional enemies – weeds, pests and plant diseases – will multiply in the warmer conditions, which means that more chemical inputs will have to be used, or entirely new systems of crop management devised and introduced. One such environmentally friendly system (Integrated Crop Management) would involve using only small quantities of chemicals, and then only when really necessary, and leaving pest control largely to natural forces. Strips of uncultivated land about 2 m wide would be left around fields. The wild plants that would grow in these strips would encourage beneficial insects (butterflies, bees and so on) as well as pest-controlling birds. Precision farming may also play its part. This is where high-tech equipment is used to identify which cropped area needs inputs such as fertilisers or pesticide, so they can be applied in the right place and in the right quantities. Management systems such as these demand considerable financial, technological and knowledge inputs. At a time when the economy of a country is under stress, not all of these inputs may necessarily be available.

The possible impact of global warming on mechanised farming communities is less certain than that on traditional societies. While the effects of increasing temperature, greater rainfall variability and higher $CO_2$ concentrations can be predicted reasonably accurately, the capacity for the farmers to adapt is far less certain. The behavioural, economic and institutional adjustments of the farming community will vary enormously, and it will take some time for successful strategies to emerge. However, the US Environmental Protection Agency predicts that diversified farming areas will fare better than those where production is highly specialised. For example, they expect crop and livestock production in the Great Plains to be more vulnerable than the mixed farming of the northeastern seaboard of the USA.

Effects such as those shown in **7.6** may well be manageable but, given the present state of play, we can only guess as to their possible future dimensions and therefore the scale of adjustment that will be necessary to cope with them. There is an important warning here. All of our agricultural systems and the infrastructure to support them, such as levees and roads, are designed on the basis of known or experienced climate. Engineers design structures on the basis of expected conditions, using statistics derived from recent observations. If the climate shifts to such an extent that these statistics are no longer relevant, it will become necessary to reassess many of the assumptions on which our society has developed. These range from mundane issues, such as whether offices will require air-conditioning to make working conditions comfortable, to questions about whether certain crops can be grown in a region, whether insect pests will migrate to a region – posing a hazard to plant or even human health – or whether water supplies may be adequate in the future.

## Review

8 Explain why:

a An increase in global $CO_2$ concentrations may have both positive and negative impacts on world agriculture.

b Adjusting to climatic change may be more difficult for commercial farming than for subsistence farming.

| Element | Positive impact | Negative impact |
|---------|----------------|-----------------|
| Road transport | Lower maintenance costs, such as winter salting and the repair of frost-damaged road surfaces. | The buckling of roads built over permafrost areas. |
| Water transport | An increase in the ice-free season and the ability to transport goods through the Arctic Ocean. | Increased disruption due to lower water levels; for example, in the Mississippi. |
| Property (see also Chapter 8) | Less need for expensive heating and insulation in some locations. | An increased risk from fire, landslides and subsidence; and an increased need for air-conditioning in some areas. |
| Health | Beneficial effects in winter, such as lower rates of respiratory diseases and influenza. | Disruption of the health infrastructure. The spread of disease, and expansion of the range of disease-carrying pests. Increased heat-related mortality, especially in cities. |
| Energy | Less energy needed for heating purposes. | An increased demand for air-conditioning. The net balance between heating and air-conditioning would probably be an overall reduction in US fuel demand. |

**Figure 7.6** Some effects of climatic change on human settlement and industry in the USA

SECTION E

## Some other consequences

One might say that the impacts of climatic change we have considered so far in this chapter are the most obvious and predictable ones. But there will be many other, and perhaps more subtle, consequences. It has already been suggested that certain species of plant and animal will find it difficult to adapt to rapid climatic change. There is a distinct possibility that some species that have more restricted geographical ranges, and less ability than some others to spread quickly, will become extinct. In short, large areas of the globe will suffer a loss of biodiversity. In contrast, pests and diseases will be able to thrive in new parts of the world and, unless effective action is taken quickly, breeding populations of 'carrier' insects could become established outside their current range. Therefore, the global pattern of diseases such as malaria could change.

As weather patterns alter, so will landscape processes. Wetter areas may suffer from an increase in mudslides and landslips, the increased water lubricating slopes that have remained stable for centuries. In others, desiccation may lead to the failure of building foundations as the ground dries out. This could require the rebuilding or strengthening of large areas

## Review

**9** Summarise the possible positive and negative effects of climatic change on all the items in this section; that is, sea-level changes and the use of coastal areas, the exploitation of natural vegetation, agriculture and urban land use.

**10** Construct a table similar to **7.6**, to show the range of impacts likely to be experienced in the UK. You might include some new headings.

of housing. Transport will also be affected. For example, rising precipitation and temperatures will create ideal conditions for the formation of mist and fog. The migration of people may be expected to increase, particularly where climatic change makes farmland marginal, thereby encouraging even larger volumes of rural – urban migration. Think of the scale of the resulting urban problems.

If all of this creates too bleak a picture, then consider for a moment the advantages. Some regions will enjoy a more favourable climate. Farmers will be able to grow new crops, perhaps at high yields, because of the raised $CO_2$ content of the atmosphere. Tourist seasons may be extended. Other regions will have plentiful water supplies for the first time in centuries.

The content of this chapter has shown the need for countries around the world to develop monitoring systems in order to keep a keen eye on even the most subtle of climatic changes. This is the very minimum required if countries are accurately to anticipate what will be required by way of adjustment and to plan appropriate action. The future rests on much more international co-operation, which will involve the exchange of information and the joint development of predictive models. It also rests on the willingness of the more economically developed countries of the world to help those nations that lack the resources necessary to monitor, predict and plan for climatic change.

## Enquiry

**1** Use your atlas to identify other countries with large areas of low-lying coastal land. How do their prospects compare with those of Bangladesh?

**2** Although it is virtually certain that climatic change will affect the area where you live in the near future, the exact direction of that change is less predictable. One of the more likely changes for the UK is that summers will become hotter and drier. If this were the case, how would your area be affected? Try to think of the effects on water supply, gardening, buildings, transport and commerce. Write a short description of how your area would be affected by hotter, drier summers.

# Planning for change

## The planning context

In a report published in May 2000, the Department of the Environment, Transport and the Regions (DETR) assessed the costs of strengthening coastal and river defences in the UK against the rising waters likely to result from global warming. At year 2000 prices, it was estimated that an annual expenditure of £1.2 billion would be required over the next 50 years. The report was part of the UK Climate Changes Impact Programme (UKCIP). The DETR achieved its figure by conducting a cost–benefit analysis under three major headings: water resources, flooding, and buildings and infrastructure (**8.1**).

| Factor | Effect of climatic change | Decision upon which costing was based |
|---|---|---|
| Water resources | A possible lower annual precipitation and a different distribution from the present day; therefore it would be very expensive to meet growing demands by 'traditional' means (reservoirs, bulk transfers and desalinisation), since some reservoirs would have to be replaced and new ones built. | Reduce demand rather than meeting an increased demand. Use meters and recycling, and encourage changed behaviour. |
| Flooding | Great damage would be done by rising waters and more frequent 'extreme events', such as storms. Coastal erosion would increase dramatically and flooding would be common, especially in low-lying estuaries and coastal plains. | The costs of new and improved coastal defences would be very high, increasing by three or four times the current £120 million per annum to £400–600 million per annum (or £1.2 billion over 50 years). The cost of doing nothing would be far greater. |
| Buildings and infrastructure | The climate would be significantly different, and so would require buildings and infrastructure to address a new set of design parameters. | It would be more cost-effective to design completely new buildings and infrastructure than to adapt the current ones. The increased costs would be 1–5 per cent of the current budget for these items. |

**Figure 8.1** The effects of climatic change on three elements of the UK economy

The Secretary of State for the Environment at the time said:

> *The most pressing areas are those with long planning horizons such as river and coastal defence, transport networks and buildings. Implications of climate change and sea level rise in vulnerable sites are easy to imagine but there will also be subtle effects, such as changing manufacturing processes in response to warmer temperatures and water shortages.*

He went on to encourage business and industry to take account of climatic change in their long-term costings, and not to be taken by surprise. Such an approach would enable industry to stay ahead of the competition. Climatic change was a challenge rather than necessarily a threat. UKCIP concluded that 'climate change will have to become part of the currency of every decision-maker, not just the experts'. However, the non-governmental organisation Friends of the Earth (FoE) responded to the report by suggesting that the predicted costs were too low, and that not all of the consequences had been taken into account.

Cost–benefit analyses of the sort completed by UKCIP will need to be undertaken in every country of the world as the threats posed by global warming become a reality. As we have seen, the implications for low-lying Pacific island states, such as Kiribati, and for countries with extensive lowlands, such as the Netherlands and Bangladesh, will be far more drastic than those for the UK. In the near future, the problem will be revealed as one of truly global proportions. So what can be done to address the likely effects of climatic change?

If you are faced with a problem, there are three basic approaches that you can take: you can ignore it completely; you can address certain issues, coping with the effects as they arise; or you can address it head on – for example, by trying to stop it at source. To illustrate this, imagine that you have a leaking roof. You could put up with the occasional inconvenience of wet ceilings and dripping water (the 'do nothing' option); you could put buckets under the drips and patch up any obvious leaks from inside the house (a partial and short-term solution); or you could mend the roof properly. All three options have their attractions (benefits): the first is cheap, the second is immediately practical and the third is thorough. Equally, they have different associated costs. And so it is with climatic change, and with the main factor responsible for today's climatic change – emissions of greenhouse gases.

## Review

1 Check that you understand the content of **8.1**. Can you think of any other relevant factors that might be analysed in this way?

**SECTION B**

# Doing nothing

Doing nothing to stop the increase in greenhouse gases is certainly an option. In fact, it is a politically safe one. Many people would rather carry on with their current lifestyle than change their energy consumption patterns. However, doing nothing would mean that we would have to cope with whatever changes occur, as and when they come along. These will certainly include higher temperatures and increased precipitation (on a global scale), sea-level rise and environmental change. People would need to react to events such as these, but the basic underlying cause would not be tackled.

The politicians who wish to 'do something', perhaps by legislating to reduce the amount of $CO_2$ released into the atmosphere, are in fact saying to industrialists that they must accept the greater costs of new machinery and different fuel usage. At the same time, they are saying to their voters that they must use their cars less and incur the costs of better insulating their homes. Both suggestions are likely be very unpopular. Furthermore, if such actions are not internationally coordinated, the opportunity is created for some countries to grab an advantage, in the short term, by not taking any action at all. So politicians may well be tempted to take the easy way out and ignore the problem, or advocate doing nothing.

## Case study: The National Consumer Coalition

An example of a body that advocates 'doing nothing' is the National Consumer Coalition (NCC), a loose affiliation of interest groups in the USA. They run what they call a Cooler Heads Campaign, spending large amounts of money on the design of websites, setting up public meetings and generally publicising a 'do nothing' strategy (**8.2**). Very few scientists are associated with the campaign, and it owes allegiance more to current industrial and business practice than to any rational understanding of the atmospheric facts. Nevertheless, the NCC offers an approach to the problem that fits with many people's instincts; that is, to cope with any difficulties that might come along, but otherwise to carry on as normal.

**Figure 8.2** The British government introduced a 'fuel escalator' tax, which was meant to subsidise environmental improvements. In the autumn of 2000, there was a crisis as motorists revolted about high prices and blocked refineries, helping to create fuel shortages. Were British motorists guilty of wanting the government to 'do nothing' about the problem?

2 Explain why politicians may be inclined to favour a 'do nothing' policy.

3 What do you see to be the dangers of a 'do nothing' policy?

4 Explain how, if one industrial country were to do nothing to address the problem of climatic change, it might gain an advantage over those countries that had opted to do something.

In a recent statement on their website, the NCC claimed that there is growing scientific uncertainty about whether global warming reflects natural or anthropogenic (human) factors, or indeed whether global warming is occurring at all. It then lists a lot of statements from associations and interest groups to show that doing nothing would be, in their view, the only sensible option. For example, the President of the Competitive Enterprise Institute has said that a vibrant US economy offers the most secure path to a richer, cleaner, ecologically diverse planet. Imposing a poorly considered carbon-withdrawal programme on the USA would harm the poor at home and abroad, and undermine America's ability to address serious environmental and social needs.

The President of Defenders of Property Rights has said that any agreement to limit $CO_2$ production would be a threat to the property rights of all Americans, especially to owners of small businesses. Many such businesses would be forced to cease trading, because of higher food and fuel prices. She believes that there is insufficient scientific evidence linking greenhouse gas emissions and global climatic changes to support the agreement signed in Kyoto (see page 94) and that the American economy should not be subjected to such tinkering. She also argues that there is also a strong constitutional argument against the USA signing the Kyoto Protocol – namely, the Fifth Amendment to the US Constitution. This expressly forbids the Federal government from engaging in actions that destroy property rights (in this case, small businesses) without payment of just compensation.

The example of the National Consumer Coalition is not meant to imply that all American citizens take a view of global warming that is mainly governed by the possibility of personal financial inconvenience. All shades of opinion exist in all countries. In the USA, as elsewhere, there are many people in government as well as in public interest groups who do subscribe to the view that climatic change is something that is affected by human actions. So what can be done about the situation?

## Doing something

It has been shown that the Earth functions in a highly complex way as a result of interrelationships between the biosphere, hydrosphere, atmosphere and lithosphere (2.1). One way of viewing this complexity is to think of the Earth as a living organism. Anything that affects one of the Earth's interrelated spheres has consequences for the others: this is the Gaia hypothesis – see page 34. It follows from such an hypothesis that an individual's actions can affect the whole system, even though this may be on the minutest scale. In fact, Friends of the Earth (FoE) encourages individuals to acknowledge that global warming exists, that it influences the environment in many ways and that its potentially detrimental effects can be reduced by their own actions. 'Think globally, act locally' is one of their favourite slogans. This is a very positive way of looking at global environmental concerns. The coastal protection measures described in **Chapter 7** are an example of 'doing something'. Mainly for reasons of finance, government authorities are having to prioritise by distinguishing between those stretches of coast that, for various reasons, should be protected (almost at all costs) and those that might be left for nature to take its course.

The FoE booklet *Energy and Changing Climate* lists a number of ways in which people can ensure that their impact on global warming is minimised. It makes the simple point that we can all reduce climatic change by reducing the amount of energy that we use. An audit of personal energy consumption is one way to identify areas of potential savings. By doing things such as switching off unnecessary lights and not leaving appliances on standby, FoE say that we can all contribute to a more rational use of energy. For example, if all of the electrical appliances that are left on standby every day in the UK were switched off, then one large power station burning fossil fuels could be decommissioned. This would obviously reduce $CO_2$ emissions and thereby global warming. Other simple ways in which energy can be saved include boiling just the water required for a cup of tea, rather than a kettle-full of water, putting aluminium foil behind radiators to reflect the heat back into the room, draft-proofing windows and doors, and turning thermostats down by as little as 1°C.

**Figure 8.3** An energy-saving light bulb

A compact fluorescent bulb uses one-fifth of the energy of a traditional light bulb. If you were to replace the three most used bulbs in your house with energy-saving bulbs, you would stop 500 kg of carbon dioxide in a year from entering the atmosphere.

Individuals can also reduce energy use by recycling. For example, it takes 350 times more energy to make an aluminium can from bauxite than it does from recycled cans. In their houses, individuals can also ensure that they are using energy-efficient light bulbs. Beyond this, they can also choose the most energy-efficient electricity provider by referring to information such as the Green Energy League Table, produced by FoE, which explains how householders can change suppliers to get the 'greenest' deal.

If people in the UK were to insulate their houses better, then there would be a very considerable energy saving in the country as a whole. At the moment, some 8 million out of 20 million households in the country are unable to heat their homes to adequate levels in the winter because they are so poorly insulated. The associated waste of energy is enormous. Obviously, individual action could also help here, but it would be far better if a properly coordinated effort was made. The government could help, by giving grants to improve the insulation of properties. The FoE estimates that if energy-efficiency measures were applied to existing homes in the UK, this could reduce $CO_2$ emissions by 63 million tonnes a year and save an annual £2 billion. They also estimate that if the government were to instigate a comprehensive policy of incentives for energy efficiency, renewable energy and clean technologies, 250 000 new jobs would be created in the UK.

To learn more about the status of the Kyoto Protocol, see:

http://www.unfccc.int/resource/process/index.html

On a world scale, the task of reducing the output of greenhouse gases was addressed by the Kyoto Summit in 1997. This meeting brought together all nations of the world and resulted in an agreement, the Kyoto Protocol (**8.4**). This set out what individual nations would do to bring about an overall reduction in atmospheric greenhouse gas concentrations. The Kyoto Protocol required demonstrable progress to be made by 2005 and targets to be met by between 2008 and 2012. Some countries with high per capita energy use, such as the USA and the UK, were required to reduce their $CO_2$ emissions by 7 and 8 per cent respectively. It has since been recognised that the targets for some countries are unlikely to be met in such a short time. Adjusting current energy production and usage patterns needs a longer lead-time than allowed for by the Protocol. In the meantime, other ways are needed of ensuring that the global $CO_2$ reduction target is met, even if individual countries fall short.

One such way is **carbon trading**, whereby major $CO_2$ producers help poorer countries to upgrade their industrial technology. By so doing, the $CO_2$-producing country obtains **carbon credits** for its assistance, and these are then offset against the target set by the Kyoto Protocol for that country. In this way, a rich country might reach its target even though it is still producing $CO_2$ above its own allocation. Another way in which credits can be obtained is by a country investing in **sinks**; for example, by planting forests that would absorb $CO_2$. There has been some argument about whether certain countries should be allowed to use these carbon credit mechanisms as a way of avoiding having to cut their own outputs of $CO_2$. However, similar mechanisms have worked well in the past to reduce

| Article | Kyoto requirements |
|---------|-------------------|
| Article 3. Reduction targets (based on 1990 emission levels) | The mean target for the reduction of greenhouse gases is 5.2%, but there are other individual targets – for example, EU 8%, Japan 6% and New Zealand, Russia and Ukraine 0% – while Norway and Iceland can increase by 1% and Australia can increase by 8%. The USA, the largest contributor of $CO_2$, has to achieve a reduction of 7% on its 1990 levels within the period 2008–2012. Demonstrable progress must have been made by 2005. |
| Annex A. Gas coverage | The individual greenhouse gases are dealt with together as a 'basket'. The reduction targets thus allow for possible growth in some greenhouse gas emissions, as long as the overall basket declines. |
| Articles 3 and 16. Trading | Countries are allowed to trade 'gas credits'. They can sell allowances that they have not used up or bank them, so that they could use them in another year. The exact policy is evolving and it may be wise to refer to the Internet to determine the latest positions. |
| Article 3. Sinks | The protocol allows for 'sinks'. These are areas of forest, soils or agricultural land that are managed in such a way as to extract $CO_2$ from the atmosphere. The Subsidiary Body on Scientific and Technical Advice (SBSTA) will establish the 1990 levels of each of the allowable 'sinks', so that new planting, for example, can be offset against the countries' allowances. |
| Article 17. Compliance mechanism | The compliance mechanism is still under discussion. In other words, the protocol was signed without it having 'teeth'. |

**Figure 8.4** Some of the main points of the Kyoto Protocol

global emissions of sulphur dioxide, one of the principal causes of acid rain. Indeed, it seems likely that carbon trading may at the moment be the only practical way forward. Otherwise, the overall Kyoto target might well be unattainable.

The Kyoto Protocol target for the USA was a 7 per cent reduction but, given the complexity of its economy and transportation system, it was a very difficult task indeed to achieve such a reduction within a decade of the Kyoto meeting. Therefore, despite European objections, in 2000 the USA proposed to indulge in a wholesale trade of **carbon credits** with other countries. The European Union argued that the USA should be allowed to obtain no more than 50 per cent of its required savings from such traded credits. For a country that produces 25 per cent of the world's $CO_2$ emissions, that limit would still mean forcing it to make revolutionary changes in its own industrial practices. The US government recognises the potential of global warming to disrupt the world economy and create political instability. It is the world leader in climatic research, and government hearings have been held to inform its politicians about the associated challenges. Even so, a meeting at the end of 2000 failed to get agreement to the Protocol and, by this date, none of the requirements of Kyoto had the force of law.

5 Carry out your own personal audit of the ways in which you use energy. Underline in red all items that you think could be used more efficiently. Do you think that you have a part to play in reducing climatic change?

6 Evaluate the arguments for and against the system of carbon credits.

7 Can you think of ways of ensuring that individual countries meet their Kyoto Protocol targets?

8 What criteria might be used to distinguish between those stretches of coast that warrant protection from sea-level rise and those that might be abandoned to the sea?

**SECTION D**

# Acting comprehensively

Some people think that reductions in emissions, such as those required by the Kyoto Protocol, are entirely insufficient to combat climatic change. It might be a good start, but there are too many loopholes. While there is no one single measure that can be taken to ensure a comprehensive solution to the global warming scenario, there are several ways in which the causes can be addressed more thoroughly than they are at present and the impacts reduced. The target area is energy, because it is energy use that is currently the root cause of global warming.

The most significant step that could be taken would be if nations could agree on a more demanding policy on reducing the production of greenhouse gases. Greenpeace, a campaigning environmental organisation, suggests that:

- there should be no further exploration for new sources of oil or other fossil fuels
- action should be taken immediately to support research into alternative, non-polluting sources of energy
- there should be an orderly phasing out of fossil fuels.

At the moment, oil companies continue to look for oil in difficult frontier locations such as the Arctic and the eastern Atlantic. The likelihood is that new reserves will be found and there will be great pressures on governments to reap the financial returns, including tax returns from any such finds. Certainly, the oil companies will want to recoup the costs of their explorations at a time when the Earth needs less carbon dioxide pumped into the atmosphere, not more. However, alternative sources of energy already exist and could soon contribute a lot to the reduction of $CO_2$. It has been suggested, for example, that the UK could meet a fifth or more of its energy needs from indigenous renewable resources by 2025, given the political will. This could be achieved with existing technology and would involve mainly wind energy, biofuel waste and geothermal heat, alongside minor contributions from solar, hydroelectric, tidal and wave energy.

Five main areas will have to be addressed in any comprehensive energy policy designed drastically to reduce the amounts of greenhouse gases in the atmosphere.

## 1 A cleaner and more efficient use of fossil fuels

### Case study: The energy situation in the UK

In the UK, energy is used at the rate of about 9000 petajoules (PJ) per year. This equates to over 12 500 litres of oil per person, a high figure, but much less than that for the USA, Japan and Germany, for example. At the moment, around a third of the primary energy consumption per person is entirely wasted, doing nothing more than being lost to the atmosphere. Figure **8.5** details these losses.

**Figure 8.5** Energy lost during production and use

This Sankey diagram shows that just one-third of the primary energy remains after production, distribution and inefficiency in use.

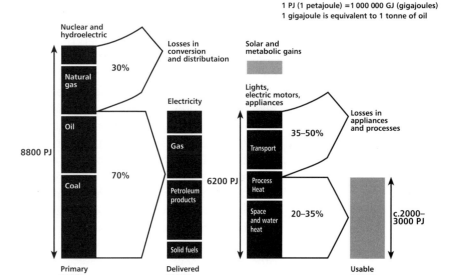

1 PJ (1 petajoule) = 1 000 000 GJ (gigajoules)
1 gigajoule is equivalent to 1 tonne of oil

By 1990, energy production cost the UK £42 billion, almost a tenth of the value of gross domestic product (GDP). This equated to £20 per week for every person in the country. There is therefore a significant economic argument for finding cheaper sources, a spur that is more likely to encourage the use of 'Green' technologies than sentiment alone. As well as this – no matter what primary source we are talking about – there is a need to improve the efficiency of energy use. In some countries – Canada and the Scandinavian countries, for example – building regulations demand much higher energy efficiency in housing than in the UK, where a lot of the housing stock is old and unimproved. About two-fifths of the energy used in the UK is used to supply heat, so improvements in that area can make a real impact on the amount of energy wasted. The other uses of energy are shown in **8.6**.

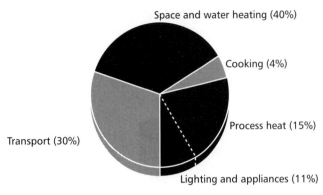

Space and water heating (40%)

Cooking (4%)

Process heat (15%)

Lighting and appliances (11%)

Transport (30%)

**Figure 8.6** The use of energy in the UK – nearly three-quarters is used in heating and transport

In the UK, road traffic produces one-fifth of the $CO_2$ pumped into the atmosphere each year. Spurred on by a degree of negative publicity, the motor vehicle manufacturers have put a lot of effort into research into cleaner engines and these are now beginning to make a difference. All cars have to conform to strict emission standards that are measured at the annual MOT test. Older and more polluting cars have had to be modified to meet these regulations. All new petrol-engined cars are now fitted with catalytic converters that cut down on the pollutants expelled by the internal combustion engine (although they actually increase the production of nitrous oxides, which are greenhouse gases). Unfortunately, catalytic converters do not begin to work until they have warmed up. Short journeys, which form a significant proportion of car movements, are therefore the most polluting. Research is continuing into new types of engine and electric vehicles.

On the other side of the equation, the UK government now imposes an environmental tax on vehicle fuel. This increases the tax on fuel on an annual basis. The original reason was to dissuade individuals and companies from using larger and less energy-efficient cars. Despite being under pressure to discontinue this fuel tax escalator, the government tax take had, in 2000, reached 83 per cent of the cost of each litre of fuel. In September 2000, a major protest against the tax, led by farmers and road haulage contractors, stopped the movement of fuel from the depots (see **8.2**). After just two days, nearly all of the petrol stations were dry. A tax introduced for environmental reasons had been effectively condemned on economic grounds. Counteracting the effects of $CO_2$ takes more than just the will to introduce potentially unpopular measures. The reasoning behind such measures must also be fully explained and the potential benefits pointed out to the electorate – otherwise, they will not be supported for long. People tend to do what is best for themselves and their families rather than what is best for the environment. They need help in order to focus on the wider picture.

## 2 Eliminating inefficient energy use

Many countries are faced with a legacy of an old and energy-inefficient power supply, housing and transport infrastructure. Some have done better than others in updating them, thereby improving fuel efficiency. Air pollution legislation goes a long way to force companies to upgrade industrial plant and use more efficient energy sources and systems. However, leaving this to individual companies has resulted in very slow progress in the past. A more thorough approach is required. One such has been suggested by FoE in a booklet entitled *The Climate Resolution*, which stresses the importance of a concerted approach involving not only central but also local government.

# 3 Combined heat and power plants

The average power station burning fossil fuels operates at an efficiency of around 35 per cent. This means that a lot of energy is wasted – much of it as heat – in the conversion of the fuel into electricity. One way of improving this situation is to use better combustion techniques, perhaps by liquefying the fuel if it is a solid, and by burning mixtures rather than one type of fuel. Even then, the efficiency rarely reaches 80 per cent and the $CO_2$ output is still very high. Another way is to utilise the 'waste' heat produced in the combustion process. In the case of the traditional large power stations, this can be done by siting manufacturing industry close by, so that it can tap directly into that heat. However, many more advantages accrue from using small-scale combined heat and power (CHP) plants.

Sited near to their manufacturing, commercial or residential customers, the CHP plants can be small and can use one of a number of fuels. Although several have been built that burn oil, natural gas or coal, they do not need to rely on fossil fuels. Many use fuels such as solid waste, straw or methane from waste tips. In addition, CHP stations typically use 30 per cent less primary fuel to obtain an output of heat and power equivalent to that from conventional power stations. As well as this, if individual boilers in manufacturing plants or domestic premises are replaced by central facilities, the outputs of nitrous oxides and sulphur, as well as of $CO_2$, are reduced. Given all their advantages, it might be expected that this form of power unit would be in extensive use. CHP plants do serve housing districts in Berlin, Copenhagen, Milan, Munich and Paris, for example, but as yet no UK cities have installed them for domestic purposes. In fact, in 2000, only 2 per cent of the UK's power was produced by CHPs.

# 4 Improving the storage of energy

Many sources of energy are intermittent and variable. In addition, a country's demand is also variable on different time-scales, and it is often difficult to match these requirements to supply. So if maximum demand is in winter, as it is in the UK, then the energy policy needs to match the maximum demand expected. This leads to inefficiency and over-capacity. If there were a way of storing the energy, then the production could be aimed at a lower figure, saving it to meet the maximum demand and helping to cut $CO_2$ output.

The traditional way of storing electrical energy is to use a battery. Great strides have been made in increasing the efficiency of batteries in recent years – as they will need to be if electric vehicles are to play a part in reducing the amount of pollution related to transport. However, batteries will only store relatively small amounts of energy. Much greater amounts can be stored by other means. Pumped storage, as in the case of the Dinorwic scheme in North Wales, is a way of storing large amounts of energy. Excess electrical power is drawn from the national grid at night to pump water from a lower reservoir to a higher one. During the day, when higher demand (and perhaps sudden demand) occurs, the water is let out of the top lake through the turbines and into the lower lake, ready to be cycled again when demand is low. This scheme generates 1700 MW of power, available to the grid very quickly.

The most frequently used method of storing low-temperature heat is to store it in water – the familiar idea behind our central-heating radiators. The same principle can be used for interseasonal storage. At Lyckebo in northern Sweden, a 4500 m² array of flat-plate solar collectors heats water that is stored in a 100 000 m³ underground (and therefore well insulated) cavern. It is then used to meet some of the heating requirements of a small settlement. We usually think of solar schemes as operating in hot countries where the Sun is much stronger (that is, higher in the sky). However, the Lyckebo scheme has been operating successfully, at a latitude similar to that of the Shetland Isles, since 1983. It is now being used as the model for much larger schemes in Sweden.

Science fiction writers have for many years predicted that hydrogen would be used as a fuel. It burns cleanly and the only by-product of combustion is water vapour. It can be manufactured from water by electrolysis, is simple to store and can be transported easily. However, it is very volatile and the amount of energy stored per unit volume of hydrogen is relatively low. Production costs are relatively high as well, but it is another way of storing energy. It could be produced by using solar cells during the summer and stored for burning in the winter. If the costs can be reduced and safety increased, this non-polluting fuel could play a part in a cleaner future.

## 5 Alternative sources of energy

Clean methods of producing electricity are already with us. They are summarised in **8.7** and more detail can be found in a companion volume to this book, *Natural Resources, Their Use and Abuse* by David Elcome. The energy sources listed in **8.7** are capable of satisfying our demands, but many are currently seen by planners as alternative rather than mainstream producers. The potential for reducing carbon dioxide output is one driving force that is likely to make them more attractive to consumers. Governments have started to apply preferential taxes, making electricity produced by these means cheaper. As fossil resources begin to run out, countries will be forced to look at alternative sources. It is a telling sign that companies such as BP and Shell, traditionally producers of hydrocarbon fuels, are now actively engaged in research into new technologies such as solar power. When major companies start to look seriously at the technology of alternative energy, then prices will start to come down and such energy will become more of a serious contender.

While the production of energy without adding to the greenhouse gases in the atmosphere may be achieved within the next 30 years, the concentrations already there need also to be decreased. As we have seen, plants use carbon dioxide in the process of photosynthesis. Therefore, a large-scale reforestation programme would help to **sequester** the gas (remove it from the atmosphere), a process encouraged by the Kyoto

**Figure 8.7** A summary of the main clean sources of energy

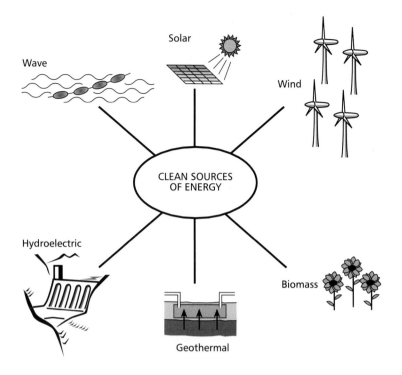

Protocol. Unfortunately, the current rate of deforestation in the world in areas such as the Amazon and Malaysia is much greater than the rate of new planting.

Some scientists have suggested that it might be possible to enhance the ability of phytoplankton growth in the oceans to sequester $CO_2$. This has already been achieved, on an experimental basis, by seeding a nutrient-poor region of the Pacific Ocean with iron. In 1995, one ton of iron powder was spread across the surface waters of the ocean near to the Galapagos Islands. Within a week, this had encouraged a phytoplankton bloom over an area of some 60 km². Unfortunately, the response of the phytoplankton did not last and the bloom died after a further week. Nevertheless, the experiment demonstrated that if such blooms could be routinely produced, the sequestering effect might be more long-lasting and effective. However, researchers at the Plymouth Marine Laboratory, which carried out the Galapagos experiment, said that it would be 'ecological vandalism' to use the technique on a large scale under present conditions. While it could provide a very useful emergency technique, the ecological effects on the ocean as a whole are quite uncertain and might not be positive.

A major contribution can be made to the global situation by individual countries addressing one or more of these items, but the sort of global impact that is required will only be achieved when the political will is displayed to implement all of them on a world scale. There are great costs involved, but the global community has to decide whether a 'do nothing' or a piecemeal 'do something' approach will make enough impact, or whether climatic change is serious enough to warrant a more comprehensive approach. In order for countries to comply with a comprehensive approach, much more stringent requirements would certainly be called for – and there can be no doubting that this is what is needed. In fact, if we do not start to take serious action soon, it is probable that we will have no choice.

## Review

**9** Explain why only one-third of the potential energy available to the UK is converted into energy.

**10** What are the advantages of providing heat and power to a large housing estate by a CHP rather than by traditional means?

**11** How might the losses in current UK energy use be reduced?

**12** Explain how energy storage cuts down on the production of $CO_2$.

**13** Critically examine the three options outlined in this chapter for dealing with global warming. Make a list of the advantages and drawbacks of each.

SECTION E

## Conclusion

Comprehensive planning is badly needed to tackle the worst problems that are likely to arise as a result of global warming. The problems are not confined within the borders of individual countries. They are truly global problems. Global institutions have started to address them. For instance, the Intergovernmental Panel on Climate Change (IPCC) was set up by the United Nations in 1988 for this very purpose. The Kyoto Summit of 1997 demonstrated how important global warming is now seen to be, but there is as yet a vast gap between the talking and the action. If the forecasts of global climate models are correct, the climate that you can expect in 20 years' time will be very different from the one experienced now. It will be a lot warmer. It could be wetter or drier, depending on where you are on the planet. Climatic extremes will be much more frequent. The news media will be full of stories of environmental disasters and associated political problems. In other words, uncertainty will increase.

This book has outlined some of the causes of this growing uncertainty about global warming and the climatic future. It has also shown what needs to be done to address the situation. The common need for people in all parts of the world to respond to the inevitable disruptions caused by global warming may yet serve to unite us in dealing with a challenge of truly global proportions.

## Enquiry

1   How would you set about encouraging individuals to play a part in any national programme for the reduction of energy use? Think about education, encouragement and legal obligation.

2   Find out the latest state of play as far as reaching the Kyoto emission reduction targets is concerned (see website).

3   'To stop climate change altogether is not possible. The equation is more one of slowing down the scale and speed of climate change to one which the Earth's human and ecological systems appear to be able to adapt' (FoE). To what extent do you agree with this statement? Wherever possible, use actual examples to support your argument.

   a   The Montreal Protocol (**Chapter 5 Section F**) is a model for the way in which a potential environmental disaster has been averted by concerted action. Do you think a similar agreement on restricting the emissions of greenhouse gases is desirable, and is it enforceable? (In particular, do you think that the newly industrialising countries such as China should be restricted in the type and amount of energy they use?)
   b   An alternative would be to try to live with the effects of climatic change. Which is better: enforcing pollution laws or adapting to change?

# Further reading and resources

We have checked all of them, so that you can have some guarantee of the quality of the data they contain. Another interesting non-governmental site that we have checked out is:

http://www.climatehotmap.org/euroruss.html

This gives very interesting ideas about how climate might change throughout the world. These are various authors' best guesses, but are very instructive regarding the range of challenges that we might be about to face.

Do not worry if you do not have Internet access. The daily and Sunday newspapers frequently contain articles on global warming and climatic change, as do magazines such as *New Scientist*, *New Internationalist* and *Ecology*.

Amongst the books that you might refer to are the following:

Michael Witherick *et al.*, *Environment and People*, Stanley Thornes (Publishers) Ltd, 1995.

David Elcome, *The Fragile Environment: Pollution and Abuse*, Stanley Thornes (Publishers) Ltd, 1999.

John Houghton, *Global Warming*, Cambridge University Press, 1994.

William K. Stevens, *The Change in the Weather: People, Weather, and the Science of Climate*, Delacorte Press, 1999.

S. George H. Philander, *Is the Temperature Rising? The Uncertain Science of Global Warming*, Princeton University Press, 2000.

Andrew S. Goudie and Heather Viles, *The Earth Transformed: an Introduction to Human Impacts on the Environment*, Blackwell, 1997.

Thomas M. Cronin, *Principles of Paleoclimatology*, Columbia University Press, 1999.

Neil Roberts, *The Holocene: an Environmental History*, Blackwell, 1998.

Richard C. L. Wilson, Stephen A. Drury and J. L. Chapman, *The Great Ice Age*, Open University/Routledge, 2000.

Those of you who would like to follow up in greater detail some of the more scientific aspects of interpreting the evidence of past climatic changes could refer to these books by one of the authors of this title:

Raymond S. Bradley, *Paleoclimatology: Reconstructing Climates of the Quaternary*, Academic Press, 1999.

Raymond S. Bradley and Philip D. Jones, *Climate Since A.D. 1500*, Routledge, 1995.